BETWEEN THE VALLEY AND THE MOUNTAINTOP

GLIMPSES OF GOD IN THE MIDDLE PLACES

Janet Reeger Hines

LIFEWISE BOOKS

BETWEEN THE VALLEY & THE MOUNTAINTOP
GLIMPSES OF GOD IN THE MIDDLE PLACES
BY JANET REEGER HINES

Copyright © 2019 Janet Reeger Hines. All rights reserved. Except for brief quotations for review purposes, no part of this book may be reproduced in any form without prior written permission from the author.

Published by:
LIFEWISE BOOKS
PO BOX 1072
Pinehurst, TX 77362
LifeWiseBooks.com

Cover Design and Interior Layout | Yvonne Parks | PearCreative.ca
To contact the author | www.JanetHines.com

ISBN (Print): 978-1-947279-81-0
ISBN (eBook): 978-1-947279-82-7

DEDICATION

God has given me the gift of seeing pain in others because of my own experience with pain. We put forth so much energy and work so hard to cover our shame, regret, betrayal and fear without realizing these emotions hold us prisoner because we give them that power over us. I see the tired eyes from sleepless nights, the sagging shoulders tired from carrying all that weight and the weary feet tired from walking alone. I see past the mask of success, the thrill of power and achievement, to the heart that knows there must be more to this life. I dedicate this book to you.

I promise you are seen; your heart's deepest pain can be laid at Jesus' feet and your burdens can be handed over to Jesus who is waiting as you learn a new rhythm of walking with Him by your side. No one would consider climbing out of the valleys to the big mountains we face without a guide. This is the space where I met God and learned to trust Him and He became the guide I had been looking for all my life. Welcome to the adventure. Let's continue this journey together. This is for you.

SPECIAL ACKNOWLEDGEMENTS

To my mentors: Laura, Cynthia. Kari and Sarah – Your patience with me has been nothing short of miraculous. You never let me give up.

To Denise – Thank you for believing in me from day one.

To Christa – Thank you for teaching me how to get my ducks in a row.

To my children and grandchildren – I pray you learn to make peace with what life brings your way. Remember God loves you, and so do I. Never, ever give up and never quit the journey.

CONTENTS

Introduction	11
Fixing Things	15
Broken, Needing Healing	23
Beginnings	27
Choosing Wisely	35
Remember This	43
When My Is Becomes My Was	51
Goals	59
Glimpses Of	65
Behold	71
Open Ears and Open Hands	77
Write My Story	85
Rising Happy	91
VIP	97
Options	105
Run Little One	111
God Waits on High	117
Walking with Grandpa	125
I Want to Be Like a Tree	131
The Moon	137

Smiling Eyes	143
Ripples in the Reflections	151
As We Walk Away	157
Mile Markers	165
Beauty Rest	173
Tide's Out	179
God is Love	187
Finishing	195
Rhythms and Reflections	201
Fear Not	207
Love Like Him	215
Name That Funk	221
What I Learned from a Can of Tuna…and My Grandson	227
It is Well	235
Conclusion	243
About the Author	247
Works Cited	249

"With my whole heart I cry; answer me, O Lord! I will keep your statutes. I call to you; save me, that I may observe your testimonies. I rise before dawn and cry for help; I hope in your words. My eyes are awake before the watches of the night, that I may meditate on your promise. Hear my voice according to your steadfast love; O Lord, according to your justice give me life."
Psalm 119:145-149 ESV

INTRODUCTION

Life over six decades has taken me on an incredible journey of discovery. Traveling through the darkest of days in the depths of loss and rejection, my spirit gave in to hopelessness. Determined not to stay in that place, I set out to find the greatest heights of redemption—a joy-filled and grace-filled life—and found God in every space between.

The short stories in this book share a few of my meaningful encounters with darkness (absence of God) and the full light (the kind only God can bring). I pray you learn to see God in the midst of your journey whether you are in a dark season, emerging from one, or living in full light with God up close and personal.

Struggling through disasters like hurricane Katrina, divorce, death, drug addictions, and serious mental health challenges, our family has encountered many very dark days. Before these dark days, we casually spoke of the light. Since those days, we still speak of the light but we authentically speak of the depths of darkness we passed through, the transformation we experienced there and the brilliance of the Light we now live in.

Our goal in this community you have chosen to join as you read this book is to stay as close and personal as possible to Him as we climb the mountains and descend into the valleys—always with God as our guide on the journey with us.

Life is a journey of ups and downs until the day we no longer walk this earth and join Him in our eternal home. Come, walk with us in a community of fellow explorers seeking God in places deeper than we have ever been before.

I am not a professional counselor or a theologian. I am a woman who loves God. Patiently, He has shown me that the road I'm traveling (and sharing its many valuable lessons) can help other travelers as well. My hope is for each of us to live the life God has uniquely designed for us.

I pray you are led to a place where you can trust yourself to face the darkness as you realize you are never alone when God is with you. Coming through these times and emerging into the light with great joy makes this journey worth it. If you have experienced this healing, rejoice with us and join us as we share the Light of Jesus with this world.

Father, come close to each heart that reads this book. Join us in our journey. Show us Your presence in the world around us. Show up in our lives as we struggle to learn a new way. We want to follow You, Lord. We praise You in our storms and we want to live the rest of our days walking hand in hand with You. Amen.

"I rise before dawn and cry for help; I hope in your words"
Psalm 119:147 ESV

This sweet spot is right around the corner from my house. I come here often to watch the Tchefuncte River slowly make its way south to Lake Ponchartrain. It is a place undisturbed while the fishermen are all out fishing. Even the still water reflects the blue skies above.

Chapter One
FIXING THINGS

Often when someone facing a crisis calls me, my first response is to think of how we can "fix it." What can instantly be done to help, intercede, or provide guidance through the crisis? How can we make this go away, so we can resume our normal life? Seeking to quickly move past this bump in the road and make it a just temporary inconvenience, we can assist to remove its power over a life.

But the past few years have taught me a deeper truth. Time, money, jumping in with both feet to solve the crisis or even avert the crisis, is not the "best" way. Going for a quick fix is not even close when we believe God is our sovereign God. When we, as His precious children, believe every word written in scripture, and the red letters representing Jesus' words are written on our hearts, we do have a better option. Prayer.

It's no secret that we want to help, *BUT*, when we respond before praying, we are not giving our best. No matter how much we love the person calling us, sitting across the table or walking beside us, if we don't first speak with God, we are not giving our best. Hundreds of scriptures assure us God is listening. He tells us repeatedly how much He loves us. We only need to speak our fears, worries, and anxieties to Him and He welcomes us with open arms. (And often says, "Finally!") He wants us to bring this life of struggle to Him. This can be done silently or verbally. Occasionally, screaming may even come into play.

THE PHONE CALL YOU NEVER WANT TO RECEIVE

One Sunday afternoon, my then forty-year-old son called me in a panic. "Mom, Reid and I just had a wreck! Mom, it is so bad!" It was awful. I started praying, then called my pastor and we prayed together. When my son called me back, I connected the three of us and we continued to pray.

I barely remember driving the three miles to the scene. As traffic backed up, I pulled to the side of the road, parked and began running toward the scene. Hugging my son tightly, I turned and took my five-year-old grandson from his aunt who was already there. I sat down on the hot asphalt rocking him and giving God all my praise. "Nana, I was really scared, I cried." We talked about the angels protecting him as I kept erupting into bursts of grateful prayer. I felt the overwhelming presence of God. I still cry as I write this. There was not one single part of this where I was in control of anything except how I chose to respond. Once again, I knew I couldn't do this life without God. Thankfully their injuries weren't serious enough for them to be hospitalized.

For almost 60 years, I tried to rush in to fix problems in my life—often due to my desire to make them go away. I didn't want to deal with them. Attempting to be in such control, I missed many lessons and opportunities to experience God working in my life.

My "I can do this myself" challenges kept me focused on the horizon, constantly looking around for what I "needed" to do. In desperation, I decided to find out for myself how life would change if I offered my prayers, lifting these problems vertically to our God. I began to see Him answer my prayers. Prayers for wisdom. Prayers for the ability to forgive. Prayers for something to change in my life. Changes began to be noticeable, even changes in myself. I began to respond differently. I began sleeping better and no longer went to bed overwhelmed at night. Knowing God was listening and I was heard was a comfort my heart had long been searching for.

I have become more intentional in this as I see how life and living is definitely out of my control. I don't like feeling helpless. Do you? And that, my friends, has become the trigger initiating my prayer response. Communication with God has become my first response.

My journey over the past years has led me down through deep, dark valleys and over steep and treacherous mountaintops. When my "I can do this myself" attitude is laid aside, one of the beautiful things I see is how God takes away my sorrow when He is present in my heart. I was afraid of letting go of what I had held on to for decades because, for some reason, there was comfort in old familiar habits.

When He takes our sorrow, He gives joy.
When He takes our pain, He brings healing.
When He takes sadness, He gives gladness.
When He takes brokenness, He brings wholeness.

What I didn't expect is that He always replaces what was taken away with something amazing. When God comes into our lives, we can expect and believe a new normal will develop.

> *"Therefore, if anyone is in Christ, the new creation has come. The old has gone, the new is here!" 2 Corinthians 5:17 NIV*

> *"But the fruit of the Spirit is love, joy, peace, patience, kindness, goodness, faithfulness." Galatians 5:22 ESV*

> *"For you shall go out in joy and be led forth in peace; the mountains and the hills before you shall break*

forth into singing, and all the trees of the field shall clap their hands." Isaiah 55:12 ESV

Let's sing and rejoice in the beauty of the newness of life which God freely showers over us. To Him be the glory.

I encourage you today to face everything that feeds your anxious thoughts, your fears, and that crummy feeling of being helpless. Can you freely and so easily bring all that to God? I finally had to make a list because there was a lot of things that kept me so wound up inside that I forgot God. Because of this list, I can now look back and see God's victory in so many areas of my life. As He took those things that kept me separated from Him, He replaced them with new thoughts and convictions that keep me close to Him.

> The beauty of a list of problems handed to God is that it can be a launch pad for a list of gratitude as we watch the problems fade. We grow closer to Him, climbing past the human challenges we face into the spiritual connections He offers.

"I can do all things through Him who strengthens me!" Philippians 4:13 ESV

"Come to me, all who labor and are heavy laden, and I will give you rest. Take my yoke upon you, and learn from me, for I am gentle and lowly in heart, and you

will find rest for your souls. For my yoke is easy, and my burden is light." Matthew 11:28-30 ESV

"Do not be anxious about anything, but in everything by prayer and supplication with thanksgiving let your requests be made known to God." Philippians 4:6 ESV

And I repeat, I cannot do this life without God.

> Lord, we come to ask for Your help as we seek the best response to crises in our lives. How can we make the best decisions? We are asking for Your help to bring our response to every situation to You first. We praise You, Lord, for Your wisdom and guidance. We thank You for sending Your Son to earth and for the Holy Spirit that resides in us today. We love You. In Jesus' name. Amen.

Glimpses & Reflections

1. What anxious thoughts can you give to God today?

2. What area do you try to control but know it is not in your power?

3. Write a scripture that speaks to each of your answers.

Lake McDonald sits in Glacier National Park just outside of Whitefish, Montana. This foggy day blocked the usual view of the mountains just ahead. Often the trauma of life blocks what lies just ahead on our path. With God, we can always be assured He knows our future. When we place ourselves in His hands, we can trust. I wrote this poem on a day when so much of the world I trusted in came crashing down around me. Not on one level but on many. I struggled to breathe and the tears wouldn't even come. All I could do was write because no words coming from my mouth made any sense.

Chapter 2
BROKEN, NEEDING HEALING

Hear my heart, oh Lord!
Betrayal appears on the horizon—again.
Sounds of trust shattering fills my ears.
Truth attempts to poke its head through the piles around me.
Deceit. Lies. Fear. Distrust. Mistrust. Broken trust.
The truth tries to rise through the debris like leavened bread in a cold room.
It begins reaching toward my heart. Slowly—so very slow—much too slow.
Truth requires trust yet I'm not sure I can.
The dark night keeps me a prisoner.
I listen as it whispers, "This is the last time."
Never again will I trust.
Am I broken beyond repair?
Volcanoes erupt from deep within.
Destruction, like lava, chases its victim.

Carrying away families, friendships and trust.
Early, dawn begins her trek,
She listened patiently as the dark hours wove despair in my heart.
With great anxiety, I reached for the curtains,
Pulling them back in my room and in my heart.
Dawn becomes stronger—emerging strong—turning into day;
Powerful sunlight chases the waning darkness from me,
Releasing me into the hope of a new day.

I remember how Jesus left His heavenly life
Came to earth.
This broken sphere moving through the galaxies.
He came here. To us.
From the prophets of old, God spoke of trust.
He told us,
Then He showed us.
He walked the dusty roads, bringing hope.
He spoke the words of grace, mercy, and trust.
Forgiveness wove through the hearts of the crowds,
Messages of beginning anew. Born new. Again.
A new life He spoke of.
On the foundation of heavenly realms.
And hearts were broken and made—new.
Lord, Your hand lifts my head to gaze into Your eyes.
Where I see the stories of Your betrayal reflected there.
You had the power to destroy your enemies.
You didn't have to be nailed to that cross.
You could have told us of your love—but instead,

You showed us.
Now, you hold me and whisper that You understand.
Betrayal, broken trust, and my grieving heart sighs.

And as I exhale brokenness, You give me new life to breathe.
New hope. New promise of never walking alone again.
I came upon another standing in the shards of their brokenness.
And I don't turn away, shielding myself for fear of my own breaking.
I come close and I whisper,
"Let me show you where to find the grace, mercy, forgiveness, and healing.
Let me introduce you to the mighty Healer, restorer of broken and new life."
Hear my heart, oh Lord!
I turn to You, Lord, knowing just where to find You,
Waiting to carry my burdens, my fears, and my cries.
And my healed scars become a badge of courage,
Reminding me of the promises You have kept.
Walking my journey with You by my side,
I believe. I hope. I trust in You, my Lord.

I know You heard.

My preferred seat is by the window. Clouds amaze me and I know I will never see the same cloud twice. Just like God's promises to me, I know the ways He will show up are as numerous as the endless clouds floating by.

Chapter 3
BEGINNINGS

"Let me hear in the morning of your steadfast love, for in you I trust. Make me know the way I should go, for to you I lift up my soul."
Psalm 143:8 ESV

My stubborn German blood refused to believe I couldn't fix what was going on when hard times came. The same scenario BEGAN unfolding over and over in my thoughts. The same questions haunting me on a relentless repeat cycle.

My energy BEGAN to wane. I tried harder. Exhaustion set in. Only when I had nothing left to give did I even consider I had been doing life wrong in so many ways. Growing up in church all my life failed to yield answers I needed today. Nothing was working. Failure loomed inevitable.

Nothing was making sense anymore. My entire belief structure seemed to be crumbling. Did you grow up without "church" or were you born into "church"? Either way, when we come face to face with our failing ideology, we realize what we thought was real was actually a façade we hid behind that no longer offers protection. Worldly success fails to bring peace to our souls. Religious rule-following can leave us empty when our lives face the uncertainty of the unknown.

My marriage was falling apart. I had lost one church family and worried about losing a second. I couldn't make sense of anything in my life. I had nowhere to turn. My adult children, lost in their own grief, couldn't help.

One Sunday morning, a woman in church asked how I was doing. "I don't know!" I cried. "I have followed all the rules for being a good Christian woman and yet here I am!" The reaction on her face said it all. I saw shock that I really believed that and then sadness because I did. She turned and walked away.

As I write this, my heart aches for my "old self", a woman I barely recognize today, the one who stood in my shoes that day. I remember her pain, and I remember how that pain changed me. God gently nudged me toward a new beginning, guiding me onto a new path and unexpected adventure as I joined Him there.

OPEN MY EYES

One day, I BEGAN asking God to open my eyes, change my view of Him in my life, and stop this cycle of failure. I had to let go of so many old beliefs, old habits, and self-reliance. Studying the Bible with a new set of eyes and a new attitude, I BEGAN to see what it meant not to fear being empty of myself—my plans, my desires, and my way. I could fill myself with Jesus' truths.

Focusing hard on Jesus BEGAN to change what was going on within me. It was so hard and the battle was so fierce. Some days, I didn't like what I was learning: standing up for Jesus' truths, showing mercy, compassion, love, forgiveness where no one deserved it, recognizing I had done nothing to deserve His grace but Jesus gave it to me anyway.

A shift BEGAN to take root. Learning as I grew in my faith in Him that in the hard times I could bask in His presence in deeper ways. But this all comes with a warning: this is not a one-time deal. This becomes a way of life—a continual process of staying near God—a work in progress. It becomes faith in action. God comes near as we understand who He is to the best of our humanness, He pours out upon us and a new season BEGINS.

Way too often, life brings one challenge after another, leaving us feeling like we have no ability to choose what happens. Many years ago, a comment by one of my kids lit up my soul, "Yea, it's Sunday, we *have* to go to church."

I responded, "We don't *have* to go to church, we *get* to go to church." I can't begin to imagine life without worship or a community to share it with. It is such honor and privilege to be able to worship our living God.

Looking into circumstances in everyday life, many times we feel we are robbed of our options, and we are left feeling resentful and angry. In the last few years, I worked hard at changing my outlook to these circumstances.

> How would it change my outlook
> if I change my attitude?

My response to the "things" that make me feel helpless and angry is to find the answers that will rob the power from these circumstances. I want to replace their power with the power of my Lord and Savior. There are many times I have really had to dig deep—deeper than ever before—to be able to find and give God the opportunity. Daily, He gives me a choice. I can choose to change my attitude. I am not helpless.

And through this process, all of us can find the peace Jesus talks about—the peace that passes all understanding.

> *"And the peace of God, which surpasses all understanding, will guard your hearts and your minds in Christ Jesus." Philippians 4:7 ESV*

What if I consistently change my *"have to's"* to *"I get to's"*?

See what happened there? I took back the power helplessness had over me for a little while, and I gave it to God. Let that feeling of helplessness be the reminder to respond by turning it over to God. I pray you will find a shift in your relationship with Him as you begin to practice releasing all beliefs that keep you chained to hopelessness.

I want my heart and my mind to be guarded by God. My heart's desire is to experience the peace He promises us here.

P.S.—In full disclosure, I wrote this early one morning. I had no idea how the day was going to unfold. I felt God had me write these words to myself because He knew by end of day, I would need them. Isn't He amazing? I sit here and smile at His rich presence in my life. With my heart full of gratitude and praise, I pray they bring you comfort too.

> "The steadfast love of the Lord never ceases, His mercies never come to an end; they are new every morning; great is Your faithfulness." Lamentations 3:22-23 ESV

May each of us begin looking at our current relationship with God, and seek a new view, a fresh view of not just who we are, but whose we are. Here's to a new day. As we seek new beginnings, God brings His work of forgiveness, modeling the process to our lives. We trust Him guiding us through the confusing message of the world and we live deeper in His love. Write these three verses down and keep them close. In times when things feel unfixable, pull them out and pray their words.

> Lord, guide us and may we follow as new beginnings unfold for each of us. Let us seek a newness in our relationships with You. Stay near to us as we remember, we "get to" do life with You and we "get to" choose how we respond. Amen.

Glimpses & Reflections

1. Write about a time where your attitude affected your outlook on a situation.

2. When you exhausted yourself trying to do it all on your own, have you ever tried bringing the situation to God?

3. Write a prayer asking Him to give you the courage to change how you respond, break old habits and look for new beginnings with Him.

The new barbed wire wrapped tightly around this old fence post created an interesting contrast. It caught my eye as I was walking through a mountain village in Honduras. We were visiting women from our Mi Esperanza programs.

Chapter 4
CHOOSING WISELY

When my very precocious, intellectual and sweet granddaughter was a four-year-old, she was always asking questions. Almost without exception, the only time she wasn't asking questions was when she was asleep. I noticed an interesting rhythm to her questions. She would just keep them coming one after another. She wouldn't stop long enough to allow me to respond.

"Nana, when are we going to be home?"
"Nana, what are the chickens doing right now?"
"Nana, can I play with the chickens when we get home?"
"Nana, when are we going to be home?"
"Nana, what are Napoleon and Nola (my dogs) doing right now?"
"Can I feed them?"

You get the idea. Finally, I quit trying to respond and waited for her to pause. When she *was* listening, I did my best to give a simple answer that seemed to satisfy her. I wonder how much of the time, the scenario is the same between God and I. Exchanges occur between experiencing God, participating in life, following the nudges of the Spirit within us and learning to trust in the teachings of Jesus and the Bible.

Believing the responsibility lies within us to care for ourselves, an attitude of "I" and the "power" of me dilutes everything the scriptures teach us. This belief puts us at the center of our own universe, which is always a very unstable and dangerous place to be. The One who created this universe, the One who created each creature, and the One who offers us eternal life beyond this earthly one—there, in Him, lies the secret of living this temporary life well on this beautiful earth.

Some want to relinquish the lies of the world. Yet, some of us want to hold on to them because they have become comfortable and "safe" places of the known vs the uncomfortable space of the unknown. The questions we ask:

"Who is God?"
"Where is He?"
"Why do I care?"
"How do I know He exists?"

"Why would He love me?"
"Is there life after our short span here on earth?"

We are seeking, yet earnestly wanting to know the answers and being still long enough to discover those answers is tough. One after the other, never waiting to hear the answers—we continue to ask just like my granddaughter.

It is important, my friends, that we choose who we will trust. Who do we believe? What motivates our decisions? Where does the core of our belief system lie? How are we going to live the rest of our days? When are we going to choose? I have many scriptures I turn to when I come to the crossroads requiring me to make choices. These are just a few.

> *"Now fear the Lord and serve him with all faithfulness. Throw away the gods your ancestors worshiped beyond the Euphrates River and in Egypt, and serve the Lord. But if serving the Lord seems undesirable to you, then choose for yourselves this day whom you will serve, whether the gods your ancestors served beyond the Euphrates, or the gods of the Amorites, in whose land you are living. But as for me and my household, we will serve the Lord." Joshua 24:14-15 NIV*

> *"My son, pay attention to what I say. Listen closely to my words. Don't let them out of your sight. Keep them in your heart. They are life to those who find them. They are health to your whole body. Above everything*

else, guard your heart. It is where your life comes from." Proverbs 4:20-23 NIRV

> Being in His Word, in prayer and in community with fellow believers is the best way to deepen our connection to Him.

There are many more scriptures that speak encouragement and hope to us in our quest to understand God better. Being still and waiting on God to respond to our questions is essential for our relationship to grow. With each mountain we climb, our inner peace grows stronger and we have clearer glimpses of God's presence in our lives. It's a beautiful display of love in action.

Just like my granddaughter, we need to give pause long enough for Him to answer our questions and fill that empty space in us. And He will and He does.

Lord, may Your words we read in scripture bring us confidence as we make choices and decisions every day. Lord, please fill us with Your wisdom to become the best living witnesses of Your creation. Help us, God, to let the world around us become aware of how powerful Your love for us is. Lord, use us to show others who are seeking the higher power they have not yet found. We praise You, Lord! Thank You for being so present in our world. Thank You for forgiving our sins. I pray, Lord, that we have the courage to forgive others the way You have forgiven us. In Jesus' name. Amen.

As we grow in understanding, acknowledging God's love for us and how it can unify our hearts, minds and lives, we can be the agents of change in the world around us.

"Israel, listen to me. The Lord is our God. The Lord is the one and only God. Love the Lord your God with all your heart and with all your soul. Love him with all your strength. The commandments I give you today must be in your hearts. Make sure your children learn them. Talk about them when you are at home. Talk about them when you walk along the road. Speak about them when you go to bed. And speak about them when you get up. Write them down and tie them on your hands as a reminder. Also tie them on your foreheads. Write them on the doorframes of your houses. Also write them on your gates."
Deuteronomy 6:4-9 NIrV

Glimpses & Reflections

1. Write a prayer asking God to open your eyes to His presence in your life.

2. How have you seen evidence of God at work in you?

3. What questions do you have for God?

I forgot how much went on this week. I saw Mama Mia with my granddaughter in the Mahalia Jackson Theatre in New Orleans and the Saints won the Super Bowl! There was a celebratory parade, a Hornet's basketball game with my grandson and a Mardi Gras parade. Not to mention a trip to Cairo, Egypt with my sister.

Chapter 5
REMEMBER THIS

Facebook is good about bringing up memories from the past. This photo was nine years ago from the time I wrote this. What a year of adventures that was. Full of amazing opportunities and some of the biggest heartbreak I have ever experienced. 2010 was the hardest year of my life.

Looking back, I can see how I didn't go through divorce alone. I survived, even though there were times I wasn't sure survival was possible or an option to choose. But, that changed. If you hang around me much, you will often hear me say, "but God". The same God I had always held at arm's length showed up. It was only then that I realized how close God could come. To tell you the truth, I never thought I would become the woman I am today. I never knew how much my journey would mold and shape me, or how God would be writing my story.

If you:

- are going through hard times today,
- have reached your breaking point,
- open your eyes and the darkness is always waiting for you,
- feel you just can't face one more battle,
- think you can't bear to hear another part of the story unfold…

If you just—can't—think—anymore.

> In that place, I met the real God.
> The one and only true God.

Not the one fairy tales are made up of. Not the bad and mean one who condemned me in my broken state, pointed an accusing finger at me, made me afraid or guilty because "I failed," or painted me as a "less than." Not the one who covered me in such shame that I was unable to lift my head or look anyone in the eye. That is not my God.

My God met me in my broken state. He came closer than I knew was possible and He waited with me in the darkness and turned my world to glorious light. He held me so no more pieces broke.

And then one day, I took a step. Then another. And another. One day I realized I could face each day focusing on the Light. The darkness was losing its grip on me. God stayed with me even when people and family I thought were mine left or when shame threatened to sneak back in. My faithful God never left me for one second.

Now, my adventures continue with God always with me. I live every day, every hour, every second with His hope and joy. I praise Him continually. If you give me a chance, I will talk your ear off about Him. I want to encourage you to believe. God is so good, loving, trustworthy, hope-giving, forgiving and restoring. God will bring you freedom from whatever shame, despair and pain you might carry and will show you how it is possible to rise out of the old and reach for the new. But, God. He waits. I know, because I met Him there.

LESSONS FROM A GRANDDAUGHTER

My oldest granddaughter has taught me so much. She is compassionate, kind and gentle. Recently, we saw horses in my neighbor's pasture. I immediately pulled over and we watched them for a while. As they came closer, it was obvious one had been abused or neglected. My granddaughter's senses went into overload. She jumped out of the car and ran to the fence, meeting the horses there. She has been around horses enough to be cautious so I had no worries.

We hung out there about twenty minutes and I watched as she picked greener grass from her side of the fence and hand fed the sweet girl on the other side. No matter how old my grandkids are, I learn something every time I hang with them. I love seeing parts and pieces of who they are going to become appear. I often pray for God to give me the wisdom to speak into their circumstances.

As I watched my granddaughter gravitate to the horse in need, it reminded me of times I have seen her do the same with people. The pain she's experienced helps her understand, connect to and encourage others in pain. She has a "long row to hoe" as my mom would say. A lot of overcoming awaits. But she doesn't walk her journey alone and I am honored to walk beside her with God.

I shared my life verse with her. It took me a long time to realize I had one. It's the meaning to my life and why I tell my story.

> *"Blessed be the God and Father of our Lord Jesus Christ, the Father of mercies and God of all comfort, who comforts us in all our affliction, so that we may be able to comfort those who are in any affliction, with the comfort with which we ourselves are comforted by God. For as we share abundantly in Christ's sufferings, so through Christ we share abundantly in comfort too." 2 Corinthians 1:3-5 ESV*

Lord, thank You for how I can see Your presence in my past. In those days when I thought I wouldn't survive one more moment, I can now see how You brought evidence of Your presence into that darkness. Sometimes with people, a phone call or a scripture, but God, You showed me You were there. Thank You for being present. When all others leave us, You come close. We praise You, Lord. In Jesus' name. Amen.

As we live our lives focused on the presence of God, we change. His presence radiates from our very being. We all have access to this change.

"I will bless the Lord at all times; his praise shall continually be in my mouth. My soul makes its boast in the Lord; let the humble hear and be glad. Oh, magnify the Lord with me, and let us exalt his name together! I sought the Lord, and he answered me and delivered me from all my fears. Those who look to him are radiant, and their faces shall never be ashamed. This poor man cried, and the Lord heard him and saved him out of all his troubles. The angel of the Lord encamps around those who fear him and delivers them. Oh, taste and see that the Lord is good! Blessed is the man who takes refuge in him!"
Psalm 34:1-8 ESV

Glimpses & Reflections

1. What has been the hardest season of your life?

2. If you haven't yet seen evidence of God in that season, write a prayer here asking Him to show you where He was.

3. Create a list of times when you have experienced "but…God" moments.

Standing at an overlook above the Badlands in South Dakota, I took this picture of my granddaughter facing into the strong wind. She was mesmerized by all that she saw and felt, even as the sun was as strong as the wind. I often feel God's presence as I witness His creation at work. I look forward to being in heaven with Him for eternity.

Chapter 6

WHEN MY IS BECOMES MY WAS

Soon after we moved to Danbury, Connecticut, in 1982, a sign caught my eye in the craft store. *"Quilting classes offered by Janice- call …-…."* Our friendship took life as soon as we met. Janice's son became best friends with my kids, and we spent many of our days together. She was a master quilter. Extraordinaire. An incredibly patient teacher. I was blessed to take what I learned and teach my mom how to quilt. It became her passion the rest of her life and brought her much joy.

When I was invited to spend three weeks in Honduras in 1999, the afternoons were spent with a group of local women, and I taught them how to quilt. As they made pieces, they sold them to visiting groups from the states.

I saw how their new talent and income could change their lives.

MI ESPERANZA (MY HOPE)

Janice was always smiling when we talked about the birth of Mi Esperanza, our nonprofit organization, in Tegucigalpa, Honduras. She played a huge part by teaching me what she knew, empowering me to take that talent and share it with others. Mi Esperanza has been doing this since 2002. Teaching, sharing, and spreading the opportunity, we continue changing lives.

We both moved from Connecticut in 1984, yet saw each other many times in different parts of the country over the next 30 years. Janice was diagnosed with cancer. She fought hard for years as it came and went and came back again. The effects of it ravaged her body.

As of this writing, it has been three weeks since Janice moved to her permanent home in heaven. Her husband got in touch with me shortly after she passed to let me know her suffering had finally ended. Later, I was texting him to share my respect and love for her. The sentence began, *"Janice is such an amazing artist and..."* I stopped and began crying. I backspaced to erase the word *"is"* and painfully, slowly typed *"was."*

That moment keeps playing repeatedly in my heart since that day as tears flow relentlessly down my cheeks. The *"was"* refers to our finite human bodies. However, as eternal creatures, our *"is,"* connects our humanity to our eternity. . We know this because we live with the assurance of God's promises being true. I look at my kids and my grandchildren differently. I can't get enough hugs from them or tell them how much I love them. I know I won't always be with them here on this earth.

> It's too easy to ignore the fact that one day our status will change from "is" to "was" here on earth. As God's children, we know that "is" will be our permanent status in eternity.

My friend, Janice, had the assurance of eternal life. I was there when she was baptized and saw her serve faithfully her entire life. She loved well. As a child of God living my life in His grace, forgiveness, and redemption, I also have that confidence as His beloved daughter. There was a time *"before"* when *"I was lost. But now I am found."* Today, I live in my "is" state. My eternity is secure.

> *"Therefore, if anyone is in Christ, the new creation has come: The old has gone, the new is here!"* 2 Corinthians 5:17 NIV

It is critical for us to examine deep within ourselves what our current relationship status is with God. We never know the moment everything will change. In the blink of an eye, we could face our eternal status.

Traveling the roads of Honduras brought this truth vividly into reality one day. I witnessed the scene of a horrific accident. The visual of the tragic aftermath never leaves me. A watermelon-filled semi lost control coming around a curve and literally ran over a full bus, and 23 people died instantly. As life has distracted us and drawn us into our own drama and trauma, we can easily become lost in the frenzy of our lives while God waits for us.

We can take what we have learned from our past experiences with God and use that as a springboard to launch us into a new relationship with Him. One that will lead us to His waiting arms. Don't let your *"is"* become a *"was"* without God. I can guarantee you this isn't a "what if" option—this is a guaranteed "when" event.

A longtime friend once said to me, "Janet, I understand what you are saying, but I have to be honest, I just can't see how there is anything beyond this life. When I die I believe that is the end of me."

I stopped breathing for a moment and still pause as this conversation continues playing on repeat in my mind.

If you or someone you know have these thoughts, remember the first glimpse Moses had of God was while he was hiding in the cleft of a rock. Moses didn't even see His face. Only God's back was visible yet that was enough to change Moses. When he returned to the Israelites, they could see the light of God emanating from him. Therefore, the first prayer we should pray is for this person to see something in us that opens their heart and eyes to stop hiding from God in their version of a "cleft in the rock" and get a glimpse of God. This experience will no doubt begin a new journey for them.

As our relationship deepens with God, we too reflect His Light. We might even have the opportunity to be the first glimpse of God someone sees. It is my prayer that God's reflection in us will open doors to share and that we are prepared to reflect Him in every conversation and everyday living. Let's shine the light of Jesus to the world.

> Lord, please be patient with us. Thank You for Your willingness to let us come to You in our own free will. When that happens, Lord, we know it will be for eternity. I dream of eternity with You. I dream of my friends and family made whole again, but that wholeness begins here on earth when we accept You as our Lord and our Savior. Thank you, Lord, for the depth of Your love and the persistence of Your pursuit. May our eyes and ears be opened to the sacred presence and nearness of You. We praise You. We love You, Lord. In Jesus' name. Amen.

I remember a day when my heart was breaking. "Janet, I can assure you that I hear you." The person receiving my words didn't just hear my spoken words, he acknowledged my brokenness. This is what relationship with God is like.

"Blessed be the Lord! For he has heard the voice of my pleas for mercy. The Lord is my strength and my shield; in him my heart trusts, and I am helped; my heart exults, and with my song I give thanks to him."

Psalm 28:6-7 ESV

Glimpses & Reflections

1. What is the biggest hurdle you are ready to move past to get closer to God?

2. What would be your biggest regret if your life ended today?

3. What is one step you can take *today* toward your answer to question 2?

I took this picture on a foggy morning on a mountaintop in Honduras. I didn't realize the soccer goal was in the distance. So much of our lives are focused on what is right in front of us that we get distracted, forget to look ahead and miss important events of our future.

Chapter 7
GOALS

"But it won't be long before the weather clears and the sun shines bright! We'll see it all then, see it all as clearly as God sees us, knowing him directly just as he knows us!"
1 Corinthians 13:12 MSG

If you have lived many years on this earth, you probably have experienced numerous ups and downs. You know well the feeling of confidence when the answers you seek are clearly defined, leaving you with clarity how to proceed through the challenge facing you. But, what about when your vision is blurred and you aren't sure how to proceed? What then?

When I took this picture, I focused on the beauty of the roots of the tree. The clouds in the background heightened the drama of the tree's connection to the ground. I love the symmetry of the row of these giant ficus trees. Examining the picture closer, I noticed something in the misty background and decided I could easily edit it out. After all, my intention was to focus on the roots.

Suddenly, I realized how close I was to missing a much deeper message in this photo. I had been looking down, distracted by a wonderful shot. Yet, looking forward, what did I see? Something even better stood ahead. An object was barely visible through the clouds. It wasn't wrapped in neon lights screaming "come this way." My eyes didn't immediately focus on it. It was only when I began studying the picture that I even noticed the soccer goal ahead.

This is what screamed at me–how easy it is to be distracted by what is right in front of me and forget there is much to see and learn when I have a goal set ahead of me. I only had to lift my eyes and focus for God to reveal this Truth.

> *"If any of you need wisdom, ask God for it. He will give it to you. God gives freely to everyone. He doesn't find fault." James 1:5 NIRV*

ASK GOD

When life distracts me from the goal I have chosen to live for, I have learned to pray and seek God. If there is any wisdom I could pass on, it is this. Our world is intent on coming at us so fast that we will forget we even have a long-range goal. We will forget there is more meaning to our lives than just surviving day-to-day burdens.

> The world tries to convince us drinking out of a fire hydrant, day after day, is normal. And if our thirst doesn't get relief from this common object on the street, we should feel like a failure.

In fact, God's Word shows us Jesus knew the struggle was real. Even Jesus separated Himself to seek rest in solitude. His example is where our focus needs to be. He knew we would need His help. In these times of rest when God is holding my hand, the clouds lift and my soul knows my sights are set on the firm ground. The distractions clear, and peace fills my being. Just as the clouds rise so will our sights. With our eyes focused on God, the remainder of our days will be clear.

Join me on this journey with sights set on the ultimate goal God has designed for us, freely offers us, and desires deeply for us to accept. Here are a few of the many scriptures that give me great comfort and encouragement.

> *"I move on toward the goal to win the prize. God has appointed me to win it. The heavenly prize is Christ Jesus himself." Philippians 3:14 NIRV*

Let's look at this same scripture in The Message translation. I love reading several versions.

"I'm not saying that I have this all together, that I have it made. But I am well on my way, reaching out for Christ, who has so wondrously reached out for me. Friends, don't get me wrong: By no means do I count myself an expert in all of this, but I've got my eye on the goal, where God is beckoning us onward—to Jesus. I'm off and running, and I'm not turning back. So let's keep focused on that goal, those of us who want everything God has for us." Philippians 3:12-17 MSG

> Lord, we come to You, humble, seeking, and wanting a clear picture of the goal You have set for us. We praise You for creating us with a piece of You deep inside. We choose to nurture our relationship and grow closer to You as our goal for eternity. Please, Lord, lift our eyes to You when we feel overwhelmed by this life. Fill us with Your hope, Your peace, and Your love. We love You, Lord. In Jesus' name. Amen.

Glimpses & Reflections

1. What are two or three goals you would like to accomplish this year?

2. Do you have a plan in place to move towards these goals?

3. Write down a prayer asking God to help you with your goals and action plan.

I stopped along the side of the road one evening and watched as the brilliant colors reflected the waning sun. A beautiful fulfilling day was ending.

Chapter 8
GLIMPSES OF

My mom was struggling hard after her accident in the nursing home van. I remember one morning sitting in her hospital room. We were casually talking as she drifted off and then came back through the pain meds. During routine morning rounds, the nurse attending her was talking to us. Suddenly, she looked at me and looked at mom and back at me.

"You have the same eyes." She said.

Mom giggled, "Well, that makes sense to me!"

The nurse seemed so surprised when she realized I was mom's daughter. Mom died about a week after that. I was getting ready the other morning and heading out. The day required me to fix my hair and put on makeup. Looking in the mirror with a critic's eye, I paused and briefly saw my mom's face looking back at me. It startled me.

WE DON'T YET SEE THINGS CLEARLY

The older I get, I recognize glimpses of her—as the smile wrinkles take on their own life some days—and become her smile. (Let me get a tissue—I'll be right back.) I really miss her. And the older I get, I wonder if I reflect the presence of God within me to the world outside. I certainly want to. There is so much I don't understand. Then I read this:

> "We don't yet see things clearly. We're squinting in a fog, peering through a mist. But it won't be long before the weather clears and the sun shines bright! We'll see it all then, see it all as clearly as God sees us knowing him directly just as he knows us! But for right now, until that completeness, we have three things to do to lead us toward that consummation: Trust steadily in God, hope unswervingly, love extravagantly. And the best of the three is love." 1 Corinthians 13:12-13 MSG

I know I don't have to understand. I will rise above the confusion of the world and focus on God. I will rise out of the traps set to confine me in day to day struggles. I will rise to meet God who waits for me. Mom and I shared the same genetics and many similarities. People recognized me as her daughter. As His daughter, God created me to spend a specific time here on earth. Again, I pray people will recognize Him, my heavenly Father, in me. May we help others rise just as God helped us. May we be the love—the best love we can be.

> May we be the hand reaching out to
> those around us who are struggling
> in ways we have struggled.

Lord, we come to You truly wanting to be a godly reflection to the world around us. Please make us more like You every day. Bring us to every conversation, interaction with the world and our day to day lives at home filled with a desire to leave people remembering the good God we serve and worship. Thank You, Lord. Forgive us when we struggle and fail and give us the hope and courage to rise above the challenges we face. We love You, Lord. In Jesus' name. Amen.

Living intentionally in God's presence as He guides will lead us through every challenging valley, mountain and middle place.

"Nevertheless, I am continually with you; you hold my right hand. You guide me with your counsel, and afterward you will receive me to glory. Whom have I in heaven but you? And there is nothing on earth that I desire besides you. My flesh and my heart may fail, but God is the strength of my heart and my portion forever."
Psalm 73:23-26 ESV

Glimpses & Reflections

1. What do you see when you look in the mirror?

2. What does your life reflect?

3. What do people see when they look at you?

When I first looked at this picture, I was disappointed. The focus wasn't on the beautiful and graceful egret. The camera chose to focus instead, on the feet and the droplets of water. Then, just as the feet were connected to the water, I felt a connection to this picture in a different way. I feel like the egret, rising and yet connected to the world. I'm learning the importance of continuing to rise and the process of moving through life's struggles as they fall away like the drops of water.

Chapter 9
BEHOLD

"And we all, with unveiled face, continually seeing as in a mirror the glory of the Lord, are progressively being transformed into His image from [one degree of] glory to [even more] glory, which comes from the Lord, [who is] the Spirit."
2 Corinthians 3:18 AMP

I marvel at the idea of an unveiled face. I wash my face, brush my teeth, apply my moisturizer, sunscreen and head out the door, seldom pausing to consider the amazing me God created in His image. We are each a walking miracle. Beloved daughters and sons of the living God, meet our Creator living inside us.

SO MUCH TRAUMA

In 2005, when hurricane Katrina marched uninvited into our lives, there was so much trauma and nowhere to go to escape. Many of our own homes sustained damage but the overall need was much greater than our personal needs. We worked almost day and night. I became director of our church's disaster relief efforts which was one of the few facilities equipped to stage teams preparing to go into our Northshore community. It was several weeks until we were able to get into New Orleans.

The God-stories were coming in like rapid fire through our teams. This was way bigger than any one of us could have ever imagined. Providing food, coordinating and housing volunteers, cutting trees, setting up clinics where people could get shots, and delivering food to the 26 shelters in our parish (county) filled our first weeks. The challenges were enormous. Semi after semi appeared at our doors full of donations from around the country. Churches linked arms in unity to serve. All doctrinal differences and their boundaries receded. God was so close.

Living without those boundaries was liberating. But that unity was short lived. Division happened. People I thought I knew became strangers as our visions of serving separated us, eventually leading me to a new path.

But the loss of relationship with my church deeply affected me. Self-doubt, loss, abandonment and fear began to creep in. Our enemy knows our "triggers" and "hot buttons" better than we do as we begin to face them.

It was one of the hardest times and yet, the first time I saw God differently. My feet came out of the water as I tore away the veil I had worn for years hiding from His deep abiding love. I was launched into a stronger relationship with God. By facing my triggers, I began to see how God was at work in me as I learned how to walk again. This time I was really not alone. He was my constant companion.

> Either I had missed something my whole life or there was no truth in the words of people who convinced me to doubt my worth and question my status as God's daughter. It turns out both were true.

My enthusiasm for sharing my personal testimony regularly manifests in reaching a hand out to others I see who are in that same no man's land I existed in for several years. Feet uncommitted, neither all in nor all out. The place where we either sink deeper into the despair of what we have experienced through life's tragedies and trials or we dig in to stop the descent and rise instead into the truths waiting to be discovered when we turn to God's Word. For much of my life I withered and was wasting away. But today I live in a new hope, sanctified as a daughter of the King.

God waits for us to rise to a new life out of the old and be transformed into His image. I pray what people notice in me first are the pieces becoming more and more like

Him—not the ones I try to hide behind or the ones causing me to drag my feet.

I am still mesmerized by this picture. The sun was shining so bright at high noon—too bright for a good picture. But the best part of it is the point where the feet are still connected to the water. Only when we are courageous enough to launch with God-provided energy will we rise to the place where we can clearly see the reflection in the mirror that the world sees. The world needs to see our unveiled faces.

That part of us wanting to stay connected to the earthly will fade and the clarity we experience climbing toward God will amaze us. Like the egret, as our feet come out of the water, the reflection of our unveiled faces in the mirror are becoming more like Him.

> Lord, come close as I choose to rise above the chaos of the world to a closer relationship with You. Protect me from the unseen dangers that want me to stay connected to the world. Protect me from the chaos, Lord. These distractions that want me to take my eyes off of You are a constant challenge. Please stay near and fill me with the hope and love that You offer all Your children. In Jesus' name. Amen.

Glimpses & Reflections

1. What current struggles are keeping your feet connected to the world?

2. What changes do you need to make to unveil your face, allowing yourself and others to see God in you?

3. Do you see the evidence of God's presence in your life clearer as you deliberately look for Him every day? Describe what you found?

This time of day is known as the golden hour with photographers. The light is incredible and each photo taken will be different every few minutes. My life is like that as I live in God's presence. Gratefully, every changing moment is recorded in His beautiful book of life.

Chapter 10
OPEN EARS AND OPEN HANDS

"God, come close. Come quickly! Open your ears—it's my voice you're hearing! Treat my prayer as sweet incense rising; my raised hands are my evening prayers."
Psalm 141:1-2 MSG

When I read this Psalm of David as a prayer, I feel deeply connected to God. Inviting God to come close seems so bold, almost irreverent (and scary, if I'm honest). When I look back over my day and see how many times I failed to take the high road, I'm embarrassed. David's example here is such a comfort to me. He was a man "after God's own heart" but he was human and made mistakes. (See Acts 13:22.)

"God, it's me Janet here, calling out to You. Please treat this prayer as sweet incense rising to You." Wow, stop a moment and visualize our prayers as sweet incense rising to God's ear.

> "My raised hands are my evening prayers."

My evening prayers rising. At day's end, how often do we feel so tired we can barely crawl into bed? But this visual David shares with us of raised hands being prayers is so beautiful. The simple gesture of lifting my arms, my hands open, being humbly offered as prayer—evening prayer—is pure connection—seeking to come closer to God. No matter how many times I messed up in the past fifteen hours or so, releasing all that heaviness to His ear each evening is the true meaning of being a Christian to me.

I HAD QUESTIONS

Let me confess, there were many days when I felt a downward pull preventing me from climbing even an inch. There was a time when I almost believed I would be permanently stuck between the high road and the low road. I had yet to learn there is much to be learned while traveling the middle road on the way to the high road. One thing after another kept coming. Wave after wave swept over me, never letting up their downward spiral. These waves had more energy than I ever had. Gradually, pieces of what I had learned about God in the past began to come together. I began testing the principles I had grown up with. I made a list of my questions.

- *Can I trust God?* So many trusts have been broken in my life.
- *Does He really love me like He says He does?* I don't feel lovable.
- *Why should He care about me?* I'm only one in billions of souls that have walked this earth.
- *What do I do about all the junk in my life?* So. Much. Junk.
- *Why do you care about me, Lord?* This was such a big one for me, it made the list twice!

I had question after question yet never sensed I was being ignored. Something in me knew my pain was being heard. This list was just the beginning but it began revealing how I had put my trust, faith and hope in people. That is where the breakdown began.

In the beginning, tiny little pieces of God began appearing that offered a glimmer of hope. Maybe a random text from someone telling me they were thinking of me. Randomly meeting someone in the grocery store I hadn't seen for a while. Often, I read something that hit home—the author connecting to my quest for answers. Sermons would reveal a clue to the questions I sought answers to. The common thread weaving its way through each of these events was God.

Though the journey has been troubled, long and exhausting, I have learned that God is where I need to place my expectations, hope, trust, and love. Somewhere in the middle, between the low road and the high road, the changes began to occur and I discovered God meets me on all of them. The biggest change of all was in me. My pile of my junk began to have less power over me. I began expecting to see Him in my day to day activities and in every waking moment of the darkest nights.

The part of me that tries to keep me connected to the earthly side is fading and the clarity I experience as I rise toward God amazes me. Living on the high road is where I found joy. All praise goes to my Father who has never given up on me. Every journey through the valleys, the middle places, and the mountaintops have prepared me for the next chapters in my story. Together, let's rise as our evening prayers close each day.

> May we lift our hands to the heavens as our prayers rise tonight and lay our heads down, at peace with ourselves, resting in His forgiveness and love.

"The Sovereign Lord has given me his words of wisdom, so that I know how to comfort the weary. Morning by morning he wakens me and opens my understanding to his will." Isaiah 50:4 NIV

Father God, we come before You with hands lifted in prayer. We offer You our prayers, praise and lives. We don't want to live between the low and high road anymore. We see You at work in our lives and want You to lead us the rest of our days. We want to be a living message to the world around us as we live out our days close to You. Wake us in the morning, understanding Your will. We love You and praise You with arms raised high. In Jesus' name. Amen.

Reading scripture passages in different Bible versions creates a balance, bringing me an even deeper appreciation for the intention of the Author.

"One of the religion scholars came up. Hearing the lively exchanges of question and answer and seeing how sharp Jesus was in his answers, he put in his question: 'Which is most important of all the commandments?' Jesus said, 'The first in importance is, 'Listen, Israel: The Lord your God is one; so love the Lord God with all your passion and prayer and intelligence and energy.' And here is the second: 'Love others as well as you love yourself.' There is no other commandment that ranks with these.'"
Mark 12:38-31 MSG

Glimpses & Reflections

1. Pray with your hands raised, offering your words as sweet incense to God.

2. How do you think it changes your prayers when you pray with open, raised hands?

3. When you ask God to be with you on the high road, do you think it will be harder, easier or both? Do you feel afraid or empowered?

While exploring in local antique stores, my granddaughter and I came across this 1936 Remington typewriter. She is an avid reader and I'm passionate about writing. We love words! We made up our mind quickly to claim it as ours. I have fond memories of playing on my grandpa's typewriter which might have been the same model.

Chapter 11
WRITE MY STORY

"May the Lord lead your hearts into a full understanding and expression of the love of God and the patient endurance that comes from Christ."
2 Thessalonians 3:5 NLT

As the years pass and recede into our personal history, we can look back and see how our stories are being written. Every book in every library around the world is filled with history. But, what I'm realizing more and more, the older I get, what fills those pages of my personal history are what carried me to today.

Every experience, every conversation and every heartbreak—good and bad—has made me this Janet who writes these words. The shame, humiliation and failures fill pages. The anger, grief and the unbearable loss fill chapters. Death, divorce, drugs, and disease all wrote their pages in my book of life. The times I wrestle with God, wanting to take control of the pen He is writing my story with, the ink runs, the pages wrinkle and coffee stains become permanent residents.

ABUNDANCE, HOPE, FREEDOM AND JOY

But then, there are chapters full of discoveries as I experienced God in new ways. I realized there is an abundance when I walked with Him. There comes peace in the storms. They don't last forever but most importantly, I'm not in any storm alone. God is my guide. I've learned to reject any thought trying to convince me I am traveling solo.

The disciples were on the sea of Galilee. Mark 6 tells us the winds were strong. They were struggling. Jesus came to their boat. Jesus walked across the water but they didn't recognize Him. They thought He was a ghost. I realize how many times Jesus was near me. He came to me but I did not recognize Him. I was fearful of the "ghosts" I focused on. My focus has changed.

There is hope as I see Him working in my life as I learn to trust Him. There is freedom as He carries my burdens. I learned to be joyful. The ugly isn't pretty, but each of those experiences taught me the wisdom of turning to Him and keeping my eyes focused on Him. There is joy in submitting to my Savior. He is my joy.

My feet will follow where my eyes lead me.

> "Let your eyes look straight ahead. Keep looking right in front of you. Make level paths for your feet to walk on. Only go on ways that are firm." Proverbs 4:25-26 NIRV

Perhaps the most important piece of wisdom I carry with me—nothing is too big or too hard for Jesus who carries it all. The bigness of His love overcomes and nothing is ever too hard for Him. His love for us is so unconditional that He allowed Himself to die on that cross. For me. For you. And as our next chapter begins, we must make room for God to write the stories He has prepared for us. Join me and focus intentionally on finishing well—no matter what the days bring.

> "Don't lose your grip on Love and Loyalty. Tie them around your neck; carve their initials on your heart. Earn a reputation for living well in God's eyes and the eyes of the people. Trust God from the bottom of your heart; don't try to figure out everything on your own. Listen for God's voice in everything you do, everywhere you go;" Proverbs 3:3-7 MSG

Because God…. That's all. Because God loves us that big. His unrelenting pursuit drawing us close to Him—that is love. That knowledge we share, knowing He carries it all, His promises are big AND true, my friends. God is writing new chapters in our lives daily.

They are filled with love that never runs out or leaves and comfort that soothes the loss. A promise that He will never leave eases any grief. Reading His story in the Bible, we learn of His own deep grief, loss of relationships and betrayal. Through it all, He remains faithful to all His promises to His children.

Rise to the challenge of discovering His presence in your life. Let's finish big and loud praising His love and, most of all, loving the world around us the same way we are loved. Following His example, stay full of compassion, hope, joy and peace.

> *"God rewrote the text of my life when I opened the book of my heart to his eyes." Psalm 18:24 MSG*

> Lord, please come close. Lord, I am excited about how You will write the rest of my story. The magnitude of Your love for us is humbling and overwhelming in the best of ways. Take the pen and write to Your glory. We love You, Lord. In Jesus' name. Amen.

Glimpses & Reflections

1. Have you made peace with your past?

2. How do you see God working on your next chapter?

3. Are you ready to begin sharing your new story? *(Start with telling yourself. Write it down. Look for the threads in your past where you can see God pulling you to Him, whether or not you accepted the invitation.)*

There is a place a few miles from my home that often calls to me. Sometimes, I am able to answer and sometimes I just can't. Or I decide something else is more important and I will respond at a later time, much like the way God calls to us. Much like how we choose to answer "Here I am" or we just say "another day".

Chapter 12
RISING HAPPY

"For by grace you have been saved through faith. And this is not your own doing; it is the gift of God."
Ephesians 2:8 ESV

Life paces itself in mysterious ways. Growing up on a farm, work was never ending but our family had a lot of fun times mixed in. I married young and we had four kids in just over five years. At one point, it was babies, toddlers and running preschoolers making up our crew. And there were always a few dogs in the mix too.

There were plenty of school years, filled with church activities and sports. Then eventually, the college years arrived with kids spread around the country. Moving across country south to north to south to west and back south again kept us in a state of making new friends and experiencing new adventures.

Kids getting married and I became Nana. Life kept on. Lots of heartbreak and loss through deaths and divorces. My marriage of 36 years ended. Addiction ended my daughter's marriage. In 2013, my mother, nephew and father-in-law died. My daughter-in-law and son had another ectopic pregnancy and miscarriage—their fourth and fifth babies whom we will hold in heaven.

> Happy didn't seem to keep
> up at same the pace.

HE WAITED FOR ME

Somewhere back there, happy was lost. Peeling back the pages of time, I strived to find the happy. There were good times—before. In the span of time between then and now, it seemed like I was reading someone else's tragedy. I couldn't put it down because I wanted to get to the part where there was happy again.

I turned a page or two and saw a new relationship with a possible twinge of happy, but it seemed elusive, fading in and out again. The next time I saw it, the storyteller was stronger, more confident and bolder. I read the word "Jesus" and leaned in with anticipation. I remembered somewhere amidst the pain and loss that I forgot to keep pace with Him. Thankfully, He waited for me.

He was right where I left Him. It felt like that friend from high school you hadn't seen in forever yet you picked up your relationship right where it left off. But this time, because of the detours life brought, our relationship is so much better because Jesus knows me like no one else does. It feels different than before, more personal. I feel the transition from reading someone else's story to reading my own again, and it's good.

I see His love for me as He looks so tenderly at me. He smiles and happy catches up to me and I know I'm going to be okay. It wasn't anyone else's story I was reading. It was my own and I understand now I can't write anyone else's story for them. That's between them and God. God is the author when we turn our lives over to Him and it's a good, good story.

Now, I'm finding happy even in the hard things and learning to trust Him again. But this rhythm is a new one, written just for me by Him–the greatest Composer and Author ever. Happy times fill my life. Not because of my circumstances, but because my response to my circumstances has led me into a new relationship with God. The most important part of this message is for you to know God waits for you, too!

Lord, we thank You for meeting us here. In our past, we thought our relationship with You was good; but it pales in comparison with our relationship today. We thank You for showing up and thank You for waiting when we didn't think we needed You. Forgive us Lord. We are grateful for the joy, peace and happiness You bring into our lives. Praising You, in Jesus' name. Amen.

Glimpses & Reflections

1. Where do you see God in your life as you look back?

2. Have you experienced grief that challenged your outlook on everything you thought was true?

3. How are you working through it, and what has been the most valuable tool you have used to process your grief?

I took this picture beside the swamp near home one day at high noon. The light is bright and harsh and the snake doesn't show up well. I couldn't believe I was seeing this. The egret was so proud! He was proud of the food he caught. Understandably so. The scriptural reference to pride is much different.

Chapter 13
VIP

"Ok, everyone, listen up! This is Ms. 'X'. She brought her car into the service department a little while ago without an appointment. I know many of you had appointments scheduled for today. However, Ms. 'X' is more important than any of you and because of that, we are going to quit all work on your cars and get right on hers. Because she is—as she just reminded us—special. That's right folks. She is the most important person in this entire dealership right now. But since each of you is a VIP and she is a VIP that pretty much makes us all nothing—including Ms. 'X'. So that means I am returning to the service department now to continue working on the cars that were ahead of yours, Ms. 'X', and if you find yourself struggling with this plan, maybe your companions here can help you process your struggle and the time will pass quickly. Meanwhile, we will be in the back, working car by car."

Did you ever have an entire scenario unfold in your head and just wish you had the opportunity or courage to share? A friend shared this internal scenario with me and it really made me laugh because I think we can all identify. But later, my thoughts kept going back to the VIP comment, and to my horror, I think there might be a time or two in my life I have been Miss 'X'. (I am sure there is—and many more than once or twice, probably even recently.) I looked like this egret strutting proudly by, not realizing how repulsive the snake in my mouth was.

A Bible study I recently attended focused on Romans 12. Every scenario that unfolded in my world at that time could pretty much be reduced to the wisdom in these verses:

> "*Love must be honest and true. Hate what is evil. Hold on to what is good. Love each other deeply. Honor others more than yourselves. Never let the fire in your heart go out. Keep it alive. Serve the Lord. When you hope, be joyful. When you suffer, be patient. When you pray, be faithful. Share with God's people who are in need. Welcome others into your homes. Bless those who hurt you. Bless them, and do not call down curses on them. Be joyful with those who are joyful. Be sad with those who are sad. Agree with each other. Don't be proud. Be willing to be a friend of people who aren't*

considered important. Don't think that you are better than others." Romans 12:9-16 NIRV

I wept tears of gratitude. As Paul wrote this, the Holy Spirit inspired him. Paul knew from his personal experiences these words were true and that we, in the future, would need this wisdom and truth to encourage us as we faced similar trials.

This is why the Bible is so alive as it brings peace, joy, endurance and hope to a healthy spiritual adventure the rest of my life. Just as Paul could encourage us in the ways he had experienced encouragement, we too can pass on the encouragement we gain when we rely on the Holy Spirit and the promises of God.

> *"Give praise to the God and Father of our Lord Jesus Christ! He is the Father who gives tender love. All comfort comes from him. He comforts us in all our troubles. Now we can comfort others when they are in trouble. We ourselves have received comfort from God. We share the sufferings of Christ. We also share his comfort." 2 Corinthians 1:3-4 NIRV*

In The Message translation:

> *"All praise to the God and Father of our Master, Jesus the Messiah! Father of all mercy! God of all healing counsel! He comes alongside us when we go through hard times, and before you know it, he brings us*

alongside someone else who is going through hard times so that we can be there for that person just as God was there for us. We have plenty of hard times that come from following the Messiah, but no more so than the good times of his healing comfort—we get a full measure of that, too." 2 Corinthians 1:3-5 MSG

This has proven true in my life over and over again. Consider your journey. There is no way to truly, compassionately and sincerely comfort others unless you authentically connect to yourself. Only then can you build trust.

Authenticity reached my deep wounds. People who could speak sincerely into my pain reached my brokenness. I want to be that person to the broken showing the hope that comes from Jesus.

Only when I braved the journey into transparency, being truthful with myself about wanting a genuine relationship with God, no more façades, could I begin the transformation process that would bring me into a new view of walking with God as He guided me into a new future.

> The Holy Spirit dwelling in me led me through that maze and into the Light.

Let's come alongside each other holding out a hand. We can rise out of despair above the lies of this world and face each day renewed. Either we are all VIP's or we aren't, but we are all in this together.

> Lord, we come to You so grateful You have given us Your Word as the Bible. These scriptures show us how You would have us live. We learn how to reflect Your presence in our lives and we strive to honor You by living our lives well. Use us Lord to reach out to others. Don't allow our pain and brokenness to be wasted, Lord. Please use it to Your glory. We love You, Lord. In Jesus' name. Amen.

These are God's instructions to Joshua after Moses died. Joshua's example of faithfully following God is a beautiful reminder of His love and promises for us as well.

"Just as I was with Moses, so I will be with you. I will not leave you or forsake you. Be strong and courageous, for you shall cause this people to inherit the land that I swore to their fathers to give them. Only be strong and very courageous, being careful to do according to all the law that Moses my servant commanded you. Do not turn from it to the right hand or to the left, that you may have good success wherever you go. This Book of the Law shall not depart from your mouth, but you shall meditate on it day and night, so that you may be careful to do according to all that is written in it. For then you will make your way prosperous, and then you will have good success. Have I not commanded you? Be strong and courageous. Do not be frightened, and do not be dismayed, for the Lord your God is with you wherever you go."
Joshua 1:5-9 ESV

Glimpses & Reflections

1. Can you remember a time when you were that person in the waiting room?

2. Write the scripture that brings the most inspiration to you.

3. Can you hold out a hand to someone who is going through something you have experienced?

This cross hangs on a wall in the tiny mountain village of Ojojona, Honduras. It represents station one of the twelve stations Christ experienced in His last days.

Chapter 14

OPTIONS

Way too often life brings challenge after challenge, leaving us feeling like we have no control. Here are some examples from my life:

- When my home state was in the eye of hurricane Katrina, I had to accept it was happening. I was only able to choose how I responded.

- When my husband told me he was divorcing me, I did not have a choice. I had to accept he was gone.

- When mom was in an accident in the nursing home van, I did not get to choose how horrible her injuries were. I had to accept the situation. I was able to choose how I would respond by spending the next sixteen days loving on her before she moved on to heaven.

Slowly I learned the choice I had was how I would respond and allow the event to shape my future. In everyday life, we can sometimes feel robbed of our options, thus we become resentful and angry.

> If I change my outlook, I can change my attitude.

In the last few years, I intentionally worked hard at changing my outlook. I did make that choice. My response to situations that make me feel helpless and angry is an opportunity to replace the power of "things" with the power of my Lord and Savior. There are many times I have had to dig deep, deeper than ever before, to be able to find the courage to identify these "things" and give God the opportunity to change me. The most beautiful part of this is God lifting me out of the helplessness, up to the place He has prepared for me, and learning how to choose. I am not helpless.

Through this process, I find the peace that passes all understanding which is a huge part of me climbing out of the valleys I found myself in. If I change my "have to's" to "get to's", I take back the power helplessness had over me and give it to God.

Let that feeling of helplessness be the trigger that reminds you to respond by turning to God and handing it to Him.

I pray you will find a shift in your relationship with Him as you begin to practice this response. With God, rise to new places and new adventures. I want my heart and my mind to be guarded and guided by God and to experience the peace He promises us here:

> *"And the peace of God, which surpasses all understanding, will guard your hearts and your minds in Christ." Philippians 4:7 ESV*

PS—I wrote this early one morning. I had no idea how the day was going to unfold. I felt God gave me these words to write to myself because He knew by the end of a very rough day, I would need them. Isn't He amazing? I sit here and smile at His rich presence in my life in full gratitude.

> Lord, come close. Fill us with Your peace. Comfort us when we don't understand. Reassure us of Your presence. Teach us Your Word. Give us understanding. Show us how to live this one life we have, well. Use us as a light to the hurting and broken world. We love You, Lord. Thank You for loving us. In Jesus' name. Amen.

Sincere love is a testimony to the love and mercy of God. We can live our lives dedicated to showing the world how that love changes us. This is love in action.

"Let love be genuine. Abhor what is evil; hold fast to what is good. Love one another with brotherly affection. Outdo one another in showing honor. Do not be slothful in zeal, be fervent in spirit, serve the Lord. Rejoice in hope, be patient in tribulation, be constant in prayer. Contribute to the needs of the saints and seek to show hospitality.

"Bless those who persecute you; bless and do not curse them. Rejoice with those who rejoice, weep with those who weep. Live in harmony with one another. Do not be haughty, but associate with the lowly. Never be wise in your own sight. Repay no one evil for evil, but give thought to do what is honorable in the sight of all. If possible, so far as it depends on you, live peaceably with all. Beloved, never avenge yourselves, but leave it to the wrath of God, for it is written, "Vengeance is mine, I will repay, says the Lord." To the contrary, "if your enemy is hungry, feed him; if he is thirsty, give him something to drink; for by so doing you will heap burning coals on his head." Do not be overcome by evil, but overcome evil with good."
Romans 12:9-21 ESV

Glimpses & Reflections

1. What are some areas you currently feel helpless in where you can see how this strategy could help you?

2. How can you reframe your expectations to put the power back in God's hands rather than the situation?

3. Where will you begin? What is your first step?

This is a picture of my granddaughter at age four. She runs hard to keep up with her brother and he always watches out for her.

Chapter 15
RUN LITTLE ONE

In 1980, I was pregnant with my youngest son and seldom did anyone have ultrasounds, sonograms or growth scans done, much less 3-D or 4-D imaging. However, at my pregnant daughter-in-law's 34-week OB appointment, her doctor expressed concern regarding the size of their coming baby. She had already experienced three miscarriages and two ectopic pregnancies, so this raised concern in all of us.

They scheduled a growth scan and I offered to go with her. I had never seen such a beautiful sight as the tech guided us through what she was seeing. For those of you who have seen one of these before, bear with me as I share. Her little head, her hands…be still my heart, as her tiny heart appeared on the screen. I wasn't even aware of the tears rolling down my cheeks until one fell on my hand. Even now as I write this, the tears fall once again.

We could see her! She was sucking, her little lips moving in rhythm with her heart or so it seemed to this humble nana sitting on the side. For me, God was bigger than I had ever felt Him or seen Him before. What a miracle!

In Jeremiah 1, Jeremiah is arguing with God. He's telling God he is too young to do what God is asking of him. He is afraid, unequipped and giving God his list of excuses. (Ouch—that hits a little close to home. Both the arguing and fear.)

HE HOLDS ME CLOSE

Seeing this baby girl—safe and secure in her mama's womb—reminded me how close God holds me—the safe feeling I have when I allow all my arguments and barriers to fall down. His words in Jeremiah 1:5 guided my prayers to my grandbaby girl. I was reminded how God already knew her. He had plans for her just like He does for each of us.

God's reply to Jeremiah all those centuries ago speaks deeply to me because God has a plan for each of us.

> *"Before I shaped you in the womb, I knew all about you. Before you saw the light of day, I had holy plans for you: A prophet to the nations— that's what I had in mind for you." Jeremiah 1:5 MSG*

Towards the end of the scan, the tech explained we were looking at the umbilical cord. It showed good flow of everything that flows through there. She was completely connected to her mama. All the nutrients she needed to develop and be ready to come into this world were supplied.

I know I am connected to God in the same way. He gives me everything I need. I also recognize the importance of keeping the nutrients flowing. Any blockage or restriction of that flow deprives me of essentials I need to live—both physically in baby girl's case, and spiritually in the rest of us already born.

The final part of the scan looked at the placenta. It holds everything together. All the fluids necessary to protect her, keeping her warm and safe. It reminds me of how my loving Father holds me safe in His hands. Hands that reach out to me to guide me lovingly and filled with His presence. God's words speak to me in my heart as I read these comforting words. I am not alone in this world. I am not alone in this life. If I allow it, fear can immobilize me. Thankfully, God knows me! He knows my fears and my hopes.

It was amazing to see her in the womb. God continually reminds me of His presence in this world we live in. He continually reminds me He stands by and is readily available to help me rise above the chaos of this world as my hand reaches for His.

No matter how excited I was to hold the precious hand of my grandbaby and pray blessings over her just as I had done and still do with my older grandchildren, my prayer was for her to remain right where she was for the next six weeks.

She stayed put until the appointed time. And when the moment came, she didn't even wait for the doctor. As he was running through the halls of the hospital, the nurses had to take over. Without anyone knowing, her tiny head slipped out as I called out to the nurses. I was blessed to be standing there as the very first witness of her arrival into this world. Her safe arrival was an answer to many prayers and our lives have never been the same.

> Lord, Thank You for the assurances we have that You created us, knew us in our mother's womb and have a presence in our lives forever. We are grateful we see You in our stories and we are grateful as we watch Your story unfold in our children and grandchildren's lives. We praise You, Lord. In Jesus' name. Amen.

Glimpses & Reflections

1. What are some of the big ways you have seen God present in your life that took your breath away?

2. Have you ever felt God was asking you to do something you were afraid of doing? Have you become more focused by choosing to live in gratitude with how and where you see God in your life?

3. How are you learning to become more confident and trusting even when you don't feel equipped? How are you connecting with God in effective ways during those times? Is there something in your life you are aware of that is blocking a strong connection with God?

This picture is from one of my favorite adventures. Taken from a helicopter flying over Glacier National Park in Montana, everything about this was amazing. From low elevations where our feet stood, to the heights above the peaks of the mountains, my heart was soaring in amazement at the creation the Creator displayed here.

Chapter 16
GOD WAITS ON HIGH

"Yet the Lord longs to be gracious to you; he rises to show you compassion. For the Lord is a God of justice. Blessed are all who wait for him!"
Isaiah 30:18 NIV84

"No response is a response." I read this statement but can't remember who to credit it to. It has stuck with me all day. Once we become aware of the existence of God—we have choices to make. Curiosity might lead us to study the Bible. Wanting to make a change in our life can create a desire to change how we do life. Where do we put our trust? Our faith? Who do we depend on to comfort us? What do we turn to for comfort? Where do we go for answers?

The world is waiting with all kinds of options to lead us down dark paths. Distractions, really. If we can fill our mind with other things such as food, shopping, alcohol, drugs, sex, bad relationships with narcissistic and codependent people, then we don't have to think about "that". Maybe "that" is abuse from our past that won't let go, the helpless and hopeless feelings that are so heavy, or the rejection and failures on top of the pile. Somewhere in the midst of this life, all this darkness becomes our "normal", and, in some cases, becomes comfortable.

But God waits. He didn't create us as robots programmed to love Him because He made us. He created us as free willed humans who can choose Him or choose a life without Him. It's a weird scenario to imagine trying to force someone to love you, isn't it? Our hearts aren't made like that. We can't be forced to love.

As a child, I remember loving God. But then as I got to my mid-teens, I wasn't as sure anymore. My inability to perform like I thought I was supposed to caused me to draw back. I was relying on my human ability. It took quite a few years, even decades, to lay down the façade I was hiding behind and just let God take over.

I finally responded to what I knew was His pursuit of me because I was learning in baby steps to trust. But then the world would overwhelm me through busyness and trying to keep up with who the world told me I needed to be. I believed the lies again and accepted the failure. I lost sight of my Guide.

NAVIGATING LOSS

I've always wanted to be close to God. I would sit in church or Bible study in wonder at the new Christians who were so on fire. I never imagined that would be me. I was jealous of their passion. Then life came at me fiercely with the loss of both parents followed by many other losses and mountains of broken trust as my marriage failed. I looked around and there I stood—alone, I thought, which was exactly what the world wanted me to believe.

Any desire I once had to participate in the world fizzled. The reality was—I became still, allowing the darkness to settle in. One day, I realized the new Christians I envied had pretty bizarre stories of how God lifted them out of their darkness. I wondered if He was waiting for me. One day, there in the stillness I realized I was not alone. Finally, the noise of the world began to fade and the power it held over me grew quiet and was silenced.

At first, I believe I felt His presence. Something assured me I was not alone. Then memories began to resurface—things I had learned in church but questioned because everything I trusted in failed. Things like:

- The sacred vows of marriage being destroyed by divorce.
- The faulty shelter of the church I believed to be a safe space.

- Friendships lost that I thought would always be there.
- Betrayal of people who had been close to me.

What made me think I was capable of discerning any piece of truth based on my being so wrong about so many things?

And yet, at my core, I began to respond to God. All those years I heard the invitation to come to Him. While I tried, I didn't fully reach Him, at least not with every part of me. My weak response was really no response, and not responding hadn't worked out for me.

> I didn't let God into the places
> I needed Him the most.

Today, I am on fire. My love for God doesn't stop. It comes out of me even when I don't realize it is happening. If there is anything I desire for the rest of my life, it is that God will use me to show the world how amazing it is to be loved by Him and to finally be able to trust again. So, I respond. I rise out of the darkness. I know His hand is always there waiting for me to reach out to Him because I have learned to trust Him. Come, reach for His hand and rise. Let God become your guide. Respond in a new way, a new way that has been waiting for you.

Lord, as I read back over this story, once again my breath catches as I remember days of darkness. I remember how much pain I was in and the numbness that followed. You were faithfully waiting for me. Every promise You have ever made has come true. You taught me to trust again. I praise You and ask that You use my story You have written for Your glory. May these scenes of my life touch others and encourage them to reach out to You. I love You, Lord. In Jesus' name. Amen.

In this passage, this phrase lights up like a neon sign "Forgive as quickly and completely as the Master forgave you." This is the heart and soul of scripture, and one of my top go-to passages when life is hard.

"So, chosen by God for this new life of love, dress in the wardrobe God picked out for you: compassion, kindness, humility, quiet strength, discipline. Be even-tempered, content with second place, quick to forgive an offense. Forgive as quickly and completely as the Master forgave you. And regardless of what else you put on, wear love. It's your basic, all-purpose garment. Never be without it.

"Let the peace of Christ keep you in tune with each other, in step with each other. None of this going off and doing your own thing. And cultivate thankfulness. Let the Word of Christ—the Message—have the run of the house. Give it plenty of room in your lives. Instruct and direct one another using good common sense. And sing, sing your hearts out to God! Let every detail in your lives—words, actions, whatever—be done in the name of the Master, Jesus, thanking God the Father every step of the way."
Colossians 3:12-17 MSG

Glimpses & Reflections

1. Where is there still residue of pain or numbness where trust has been broken?

2. Write a prayer asking God to come close, take away that pain and begin the healing and restoration process out of the valley and into the Light.

3. What promise has God kept with you? Find a scripture that best describes that promise and what it means to you.

This is a picture of the road I grew up on. Leaving home never meant I would not return. Not ever knowing when that would be, I always knew the door would be open and the porch light on.

Chapter 17
WALKING WITH GRANDPA

Dressed in his blue striped overalls and carpenter's cap, Grandpa waited patiently for me. He smelled of his carpenter shop, a place of peace and refuge for me. Lunchbox—check. Coat, hat, mittens, and boots—check. Let's go! I was six years old, the oldest of five kids, and the fifth generation to grow up on our farm in rural western Pennsylvania.

Every school morning, Grandpa and I walked the dirt road from our family farm to the school bus at the crossroads. Grandpa walked to the top of the hill with me, and then watched as I walked the last half-mile on my own. When he saw me climb into the bus, he then returned home.

I needed courage to complete my two-mile-long daily adventure. In the winter, snowdrifts loomed above my head. When I heard cars race around the curve toward me,

I hurried to step aside. Barking dogs and one day, even an unfamiliar 900-pound cow frightened me.

I WAS SAFE

My return trip home each afternoon held a special reward. Getting off the bus and looking to the top of the distant hill, I saw Grandpa waiting for me, sometimes with Grandma by his side. Running up the final stretch of the hill towards him, I felt a growing sense of peace and security. I was safe.

Grandpa took my lunchbox from me as well as my worries and responsibilities from my small shoulders. His strong hand held mine firmly, lovingly. I no longer had to worry or be brave. I could rely on him to watch for cars, barking dogs, and slippery packed snow. Grandpa taught me so much on our walks and his gentle and uncomplaining spirit touched my heart and became part of me.

Over fifty years later before my mom's accident, I would head back to the farm to visit her as often as possible. She still got around but her health was slowing her down. Driving the road to the house, the memories of those walks with Grandpa come rushing at me— the rise and fall of the road that took him from my sight, the anticipation of taking his hand at the top of the hill, and my growing feeling of relief.

The uncertainties I felt on my childhood journeys reappear in my life today, in adult-size proportions. When I feel scared or overloaded, snowdrifts pile high above me and I struggle to stay upright on icy roads. I no longer see my Grandpa waiting to take my hand, but I know my Father God is waiting with His arms open wide. He promises to take the burden of my problems, my pain, and my frustrations, and make them light.

Sometimes I lose sight of Him during the rise and fall of my journey. Then I remember what I learned at a young age. If I wanted to reach Grandpa, I needed to bring myself closer to him.

> God, my Father, waits for me to stop trying to fix myself and shorten the distance between us by giving my problems to Him.

"I lift up my eyes to the hills. From where does my help come? My help comes from the Lord, who made heaven and earth." Psalm 121:1-2 ESV

Realizing that I live so vulnerable in this world makes me more determined to keep God foremost as my rock and my anchor. He is and always will be my Father standing on the hill waiting patiently for me to run to Him, give Him my burdens, and take His hand for our walk home together.

Lord, thank You for providing people in my life who point me to You. Even as a small child, I learned so much from Grandpa Wiggins. May I remember it is my privilege to be that person to others. May they see You, alive and well, in me. I love You, Lord. In Jesus' name. Amen.

Glimpses & Reflections

1. Who has been a positive influence in your life?

2. Who do you influence?

3. How can you intentionally be a better influencer in your world?

This old live oak stands in a park nearby. The massive trunk, deep roots and limbs reaching to the sky are humbling. The moss growing from its branches add to the stories I wish it could tell. Several hundred years old, the mere fact that it has survived is stunning.

Chapter 18
I WANT TO BE LIKE A TREE

"They will be called oaks of righteousness, a planting of the Lord for the display of his splendor."
Isaiah 63:1 NIV84

In the spring of my life, I am young. I learn the warmth of the sun on my face, the joy of fresh falling raindrops, and the smell of the damp earth soaking up the life-sustaining gift falling from the heavens. I am a tiny acorn that escaped the clutches of the squirrels. I grow taller and stronger as my roots reach deep into the soft soil for sustenance. Blossoms appear as the first signs of the fruit I will one day bear.

Summer arrives and, in this season, my limbs reach outward and upward. My flowers fade and my fruit matures. The summer storms that appear frequently bring strong winds and heavy rains. The force of the winds causes my roots to reach deeper for support, making me strong. The rains nurture. I am blessed in the storms and I sense God's presence.

Summer passes into fall. My fruit grows, soon ready for harvest. Deep inside the seeds that will spring to life in their own time, allowing the cycle of life to continue, are growing strong. Fall gives way to winter and fierce storms. My falling leaves are nourishing the earth while winds and oceans carry my seeds to new places. Animals bury them to survive the winter season. My fruit has passed from me into its own struggle for existence.

Winter rest is not always easy. My limbs are bare. I grow old. I no longer produce fruit myself but enjoy the privilege of watching my fruit continue the cycle of life. I see the importance of seasons in my life and what each requires of me.

FINDING SHELTER WITHIN BROKENNESS

In my back yard stands a majestic Louisiana live oak, over two hundred years old. It is full of brokenness—holes where hurricanes ripped off limbs, scars from lightning strikes and windstorms. It leans and can no longer hold itself straight. Yet, its limbs provide shelter for an untold number of squirrels, birds, and raccoons. I want my broken, leaning self to point to God who is the safe haven for the world I live in.

I continue lifting my branches towards the heavens reaching high with the song of praise that passes through me. Winds and the birds join me in worship to my Lord. May my roots grow deeper as the storms of life threaten to uproot me. As the years pass, may my limbs stay strong as I reach for the heavens, growing in my love for my Lord.

Watching the seasons pass, I realize how much I am like a tree. I have watched my children grow into their own purpose producing their own fruit. Their children bring me great joy. Watching as their seasons come and go, we each serve the same God. Our hope and our courage come from Him. The cycle of life continues.

I don't move or look like I used to. There are a lot of scars and holes in me, yet one day I will be whole again. My soul will forever look to the sky for His Light deeply connected to the roots of my faith.

> I will embrace the seasons of life here forever.
> God is my strength and my sustainer.

Lord, there is a peace in me that I recognize comes from You. Looking back over my life, I see the times I felt alone and even my broken pieces were breaking. But what I see from here is that You were with me all along. I am comforted and content. I remain crazy amazed that You love me like You do. Thank You. Forgive me when I forget, when the times fade and I look around and see the oak trees, I recognize the lies. I know to look to You. Thank You, God. In Jesus' name. Amen.

Glimpses & Reflections

1. What do you see around you that connects you and grounds you, bringing your thoughts back to God?

2. Do you look back at your life and marvel at the seasons you have been through?

3. Which ones stand out the most to you and why?

Oh, the fun I had the night I borrowed a friend's camera to take this picture.

Chapter 19

THE MOON

> *"When I consider your heavens, the work of your fingers, the moon and the stars, which you have set in place, what is man that you are mindful of him, the son of man that you care for him? You made him a little lower than the heavenly beings and crowned him with glory and honor. You made him ruler over the works of your hands; you put everything under his feet: all flocks and herds, and the beasts of the field, the birds of the air, and the fish of the sea, all that swim the paths of the seas. O Lord, our Lord, how majestic is your name in all the earth!"*
> Psalm 8:3-9 NIV84

When I took this picture with a friend's camera, it was a dream come true. I was fourteen when the first man walked on the moon. In my imagination, I was there with him. I still wonder if that dream will ever come true. Seeing the craters through the magnification of the camera lens makes it even more interesting. I can see it is not a blank canvas but full of scars and craters. The moon is beautiful!

Suddenly, I felt a deeper appreciation for all the craters in me. As the years rolled by, I've developed a profound respect for the beauty they bring to me. I've also learned that like the moon, I am not the center of the universe.

There is such beauty in knowing I'm not traveling alone. The earth carries me on her journey joined by the other planets traveling around our sun—a vital part of the immeasurable universe. We are just a speck and yet, look how much we bring to our community as we enjoy the companionship God has blessed us with.

He knew the earth needed the moon for the oceans to move and for the reflected light to shine in the darkness. We, too, are created for a purpose. Even with all our craters, we uniquely reflect the light of His presence in our lives.

We are beautifully created in our individuality and our purpose. God's presence is deeply engrained in who we, as His children, are becoming.

> *"The Spirit of God has made me; the breath of the Almighty gives me life." Job 33:4 ESV*

LEARNING TO LOVE OURSELVES

I live in gratitude for how and who God created me to be. Even with all my craters from life's happenings, I know

God's love for me is as big as the universe I dwell in. Join me in the continuing process of learning to love ourselves just as God created us, a part of this big, big universe we live in today.

Every evening the moon rises, but we can't always see it. It lives in cycles much like we do. The closer to the earth the moon comes, the less it reflects the light of the sun because the earth blocks the light. But it doesn't stay there, stuck in the darkness. The moon comes back around in the golden hours of dusk, bringing its light with it. We don't have to stay in the darkness either. When we choose to continue moving, we will find ourselves rising back into the Light.

> The closer we cling to the earth, the less we reflect the light of the Son.

It's a lot to think about. Here's to the next trip around the sun, seeking the Light, God's listening ear and the adventures that await, full of hope.

Lord, thank You for placing us on this earth full of Your creation. May we respect it. May we draw closer to You. Help us when we lose sight of the Light by reminding us to again rise into Your presence. Bring us to our knees in prayer, connecting us to You in new and deeper levels. We love You, Lord. In Jesus' name. Amen.

Glimpses & Reflections

1. When do you feel drawn to move closer to God?

2. What are your reminders to stop and look for Him?

3. What clue signals you to retreat and regroup? *(For example: fearfulness, anger, frustration or anxiety?)*

We spent the day in this beautiful community far from any city. Located in the middle of very large rice fields, the local church had been working here. The worship was spirit-filled and humbling to witness. Aren't they precious?

Chapter 20
SMILING EYES

We settled in our chairs, sitting in the middle of the rice fields, somewhere in eastern India. First, the women and children arrived and soon after, the men gathered around the edges. The smell of something burning was overwhelming. Maybe rice fields were being burned off, but the stinging air was really uncomfortable to breathe. Suddenly, the tops of the eucalyptus trees began to sway and I gratefully anticipated a reprieve, my lungs ready for a change the breeze would bring. Well, the change came but it wasn't what I expected.

The new smell was undeniably familiar. Walking through the villages, we always marvel at how clean they are compared to other areas. There is no trash. The dirt and brick paths weave between the houses. In the middle of those paths though, there is an open trench about eight inches deep and wide. Laid over the open trench are chunks of concrete about twelve by eighteen that are meant to cover the raw sewage beneath. The concrete is designed to be the path but often, when stepped on, wobbles treacherously giving the sensation of walking a tight rope. Apparently, everyone else feels the same way because to either side, the paths are worn smooth from use.

WHAT'S THAT SMELL?

Yes, the new smell was the raw sewage. No question about it. Did you ever think things were bad, and then they got worse? Smiling to myself, my senses moved on to the quiet but excited chatter of everyone coming. But everyone did not come front and center to the twenty by thirty-foot mat sewed together from empty rice sacks and laid on the dirt in front of our chairs. Here in the community gathering place, I began to notice the outliers. The people standing on the fringe, in doorways, on roofs and even behind us, where they preferred to observe instead of participate.

The worship service began and the fifty or so men, women and children sitting on the mat joined in. Smiling and joyful faces looked at us as the melody of their music filled the air. Tambourines kept the pace, and even though my mind didn't know the language, my heart connected to God in the worship. God was there in the midst of this glorious praise.

As the message was presented, people continually passed by on the path at the back. Some stopped and listened for a while, others never broke stride or looked our way. After the service ended, we were invited to the church leader's home for chai and crackers. I hung back with the women. Looking in each other's eyes was one of the first ways we connected. Seeing smiles that began in the eyes coming straight from the heart connected us.

There were so many that day. As our morning ended, we walked with our new friends holding hands and at one point, I stopped and my heart poured out. "Oh, how I wish I could just sit and talk to you for hours so we could understand each other's words. I want to know your stories and your names and your hearts."

I'm spewing all this in English and they kept nodding excitedly like they understood every word. And then they all began chattering to me, touching my arms and my hands and pouring out through smiling eyes. They, too, had much to say to me which caused us all to laugh and giggle. These bonds connected us in ways that transcend culture, location and circumstance. God created us with such love.

Even with the challenge of the smell of raw sewage as we began our day, I no longer noticed it. My senses were overwhelmed and occupied with peace and gratitude for the time spent in community with this small group of believers in a place so far from home. There was a joy deep inside us. Isn't this what a truly joyful life looks like? Among the stink and crummy stuff that happens to us, joy produces smiles from deep within us.

There will always be outliers, but my awareness of them grows. Noticing them doesn't bring them closer, but it does give me the opportunity to pray for them. May our hearts always hold space for them while they search for where they belong. I pray for the day when we connect with smiling eyes. Maybe soon.

> Compassion changes our outlook
> of the world around us.

Because I had these experiences, my gratitude is richer with praise. Being able to visit and spend time with women in their cultures, in their countries makes me a better person. Sharing God's love changes everything. My heart continues to rise in praise to God for the opportunities I have been blessed to experience.

> *"...that their hearts may be encouraged, being knit together in love, to reach all the riches of full assurance of understanding and the knowledge of God's mystery, which is Christ." Colossians 2:2 ESV*

Father, thank You for the opportunities You prepare for us to share Your message with others. We pray for boldness, clarity and opportunity whether it is across an ocean or across the street. We praise You—our good, good Father. In Jesus' name. Amen.

The joy of the Lord is our strength.

"God, the Lord, is my strength; he makes my feet like the deer's; he makes me tread on my highplaces."
Habakkuk 3:19 ESV

"Nehemiah said, "Go and enjoy some good food and sweet drinks. Send some of it to those who don't have any. This day is set apart to honor our Lord. So don't be sad. The joy of the Lord makes you strong."
Nehemiah 8:10 ESV

"The Lord is my strength and my song, and he has become my salvation; this is my God, and I will praise him, my father's God, and I will exalt him."
Exodus 15:2 ESV

Glimpses & Reflections

1. Have you ever had the opportunity to share Jesus with anyone?

2. If you have not, what keeps you from sharing His message through your life?

3. Notice the outliers around you. Write the names of at least three people you would like to talk to about Jesus. Begin praying for them regularly.

May the ripples that rock your boat be gentle. But even if they aren't, know our God is good. Our God is a stronghold in the day of trouble and He knows us—the ones seeking refuge in Him.

Chapter 21
RIPPLES IN THE REFLECTIONS

Early one morning, I drove out Lake Road which runs alongside the Tchefuncte River. It was an unusually calm morning on the river. Seldom do I catch it "glassy". I pulled over near the edge, looking for the perfect picture to go with a "reflections" post that has been on my mind. Sudden movement caught my eye and I was no longer alone and the perfect reflection vanished in the ripples. I knew immediately who disturbed my peace.

If you look closely, you can see his eyes furrowed deep under his eyebrows and the tip of his nostrils at the end of a very long snout extended just enough to retrieve the oxygen needed to stay mostly submerged in the river. Alligators are sneaky. Many times, they hang around and are never seen, but they are still watching.

It's not a far jump to apply this to our spiritual life. Alligators are predators. Seldom do they attack man without provocation. Yet, they disturb the placid scene of a life by coming in and creating ripples. No longer was my focus on the beauty of the sunrise, the creation and most of all, my Creator.

> Without noticing the predators lurking in the shadows of our lives, we are often surprised and amazed when their ripples disrupt our lives.

Even when my soul is in a place of contentment, these ripples are doing their best to break the still and calm waters there. My personal "ripples" fall into categories. The little ones that barely cause me to adjust my balance like:

- disrupted schedules changing on the fly,
- an unexpected phone call,
- being late,
- traffic,
- worrying about what others think,
- trying to decide what to eat to remain focused on my health.

Admittedly, these are small but together, they have a singular outcome—distraction. When joining forces, these ripples have the potential to turn into frustration and negativity unless I take a step back from the water to see what is really happening around me. When I take my eyes off Jesus, I struggle with an off-balance sensation as my insecurities abound. I see the eyes of the predators slowly surrounding me because they know the power of their presence in my life could be enough to cause me to lose my footing. It's like they know my weaknesses better than I do.

How can they have such power to disrupt my life? Do you feel this same challenge? I reminded myself that my confidence is in God. He is my sure footing. As His confidence courses through me, the threat of the predators diminishes.

One evening, I was sitting at the lake watching the sunset as my grandchildren threw rocks in the lake. I felt the ripples of the day gradually subside as the sun faded. It was a good feeling. I was grateful for another day. I do my best to never take a day for granted or miss a single moment of the wonder of God's creation around me. Living intentionally in my day to day life helps me rise to the hope and truths God shows me every day.

> *"The Lord is good, a stronghold in the day of trouble; he knows those who take refuge in him." Nahum 1:7 ESV*

> *"The great thing, if one can, is to stop regarding all the unpleasant things as interruptions of one's 'own,' or 'real' life. The truth is of course that what one calls the interruptions are precisely one's real life—the life God is sending one day by day."*
>
> – C.S. Lewis, *The Collected Works of C.S. Lewis*

Wow.

As I continued my drive out Lake Road, I saw how my thoughts had certainly been interrupted. These instances are a "normal" part of my life, but my focus is now on allowing my Savior to reign and take control.

> *"God didn't give us a spirit that makes us weak and fearful. He gave us a spirit that gives us power and love. It helps us control ourselves." 1 Timothy 1:7 NIRV*

> Father, we praise You. We seek You. We love You. Stay near as we unexpectedly encounter the enemy in even the smallest interruptions. May we be constantly reminded how near You walk with us. Forgive us. We love You, Lord. In Jesus' name. Amen.

Glimpses & Reflections

1. What has caused some of the ripples around you?

2. Do you have a favorite place to go when your peace is disrupted? Write about how you find your peace once again.

3. What are some new ways or strategies you could use that will bring you closer to God?

My infamous cat leaped to the top of the bookcase and made room for himself as the pot fell to the tile floor below.

Chapter 22
AS WE WALK AWAY

Things break. It's probably pretty accurate to say we have all had that miserable experience of breaking something that was precious to us. Trying to rescue it before the inevitable happened yet the sound of it shattering hurt our ears. Like in a slow-motion video—there was no stopping what gravity and my carelessness started. No one else to blame. Even worse is when something I treasure is broken by someone else.

My mom was always anxious when our family would visit certain relatives and friends. With five kids in tow, I can certainly understand. Only one time do I remember breaking something that belonged to someone else while visiting in their home. I was horrified. I was looking at the little light-catcher hanging from the lamp and watching it move the light. Mesmerized, I moved it around and around but suddenly the tiny wire broke. No one saw what happened but time stood still there for me in that moment.

For a little while, I did nothing. But I knew that wasn't right. Finally, with it lying in my hand, I cautiously approached my mom's friend and held out my hand to show her what I broke. As I began to explain, she began to laugh sweetly. She told me it was ok and she could fix it and not to worry. She instantly took the burden off of me. That was fifty years ago. Apparently, it really stuck with me. I'm amazed. My actions were forgiven but her words to me were not forgotten. This time it wasn't hurting words I remembered but a precious kindness. That old saying rings true and maybe I learned it that day. It's not what you say to people they remember—it's how they feel as they walk away from you.

> When people walk away from me, I don't want them to remember what I said. I want them to remember experiencing the same sense of joy, hope and peace that fills me to overflowing.

LINGER LONGER

What do people feel when they walk away from me? How often do I miss opportunities to encourage others? Today,

I want to walk a little slower, sit a little longer, listen more carefully and share life a lot deeper. Many times, we have the answers to our own questions, but until we open ourselves to conversation, we often fear we will add to the brokenness. By speaking to someone we trust, we give life to the question and discover we might be able to answer it for ourselves.

Jesus is our best example of this. He listened closely to people when they came to Him. Sometimes He responded with words, sometimes without. Sometimes they left His presence dancing and singing, like the lame man who was healed. Other times, they walked away grieving at what seemed to be an impossible solution. One example is the rich, young ruler. His story appears in Matthew 19, Mark 10 and Luke 18. Three times we see this young man ask Jesus a question. He did not like Jesus' response. He turned his back and walked away from Jesus.

The story of Jairus' dying daughter is also told three times by Matthew, Mark and Luke. He was simply a parent who deeply loved his only daughter. When asked to heal the child, Jesus agreed to accompany this concerned parent. On the way, a woman in the crowd touched Him and her bleeding stopped. He paused, waiting for an answer as He asked who touched Him. Finally, she confessed she had. She was healed just as Jairus' servant came to tell him his daughter had died. Jairus told Jesus not to come because she was gone. Even though Jairus thought Jesus was too late,

Jesus continued on. He entered the house and she "woke up from her sleep". The family's prayer was answered; however, it was in Jesus' timing.

I love these examples of how Jesus responded to questions and pleas. Praying with others helps me to process and see solutions that may have eluded me in the past. So, take heart. Make it your goal to pay closer attention to what's going on around you and in others whose paths cross yours. Become an observer. Take it to prayer. Share in lives around you.

Let's make it our goal to change the world around us. I pray I might always be a hand reaching out to the hurting, full of God's love, offering them healing and a hope-filled relationship with Him. How often is it possible for me to ease another's anxiety—just like Mom's friend did for me so many years ago? Many times, we can be the listening ear that helps someone work through something that has been broken.

"He heals the brokenhearted and binds up their wounds." Psalm 147:3 ESV

"The Lord is near to the brokenhearted and saves the crushed in spirit." Psalm 34:18 ESV

Lord, we thank You for coming into our brokenness, into the places so wounded we never thought survival was possible. Bring an awareness of others around us who are broken and give us opportunities to encourage them, reaching a hand out to help them rise from the broken. Lift them into a new hope and new life that includes a deep relationship with You. We love You, Lord. In Jesus' name. Amen.

Our confidence and joy must be rooted in God's love and presence in our lives.

"So we can confidently say, "The Lord is my helper; I will not fear; what can man do to me?"
Hebrews 13:6 ESV

"Behold God is my helper; the Lord is the upholder of my life."
Psalm 54:4 ESV

Glimpses & Reflections

1. Are you conscious of how people feel when they walk away from you?

2. How can you become more aware of what's going on around you and engage in ways to help others?

3. Write the names of anyone you know who is struggling with something you might have been through. Look for opportunities to reach out to them, encouraging them in ways you have been encouraged by others.

I was not driving when I took this picture (I know that went through someone's mind) . Driving conditions were not the best as we drove the 24-mile causeway connecting us to New Orleans. When our visibility was very limited, it was nice to have the mile markers to let us know how we were progressing.

Chapter 23
MILE MARKERS

Have you ever noticed a series of numbered markers along a road or boundary at intervals of one mile or occasionally, parts of a mile? What about mile markers in your life? My personal mile markers have been passing by at a decent clip these days. My car's odometer rolled past 100,000 miles. This was the first time I have owned a vehicle long enough to see that. That's a lot of road time, a lot of memories.

Carpools, soccer practices, games, tournaments, visiting family and friends, a big road trip the summer of 2017 through ten states (Mount Rushmore being our furthest point), trips to airports, babies being born, funerals—lots of life, lots of mile markers. I've been to 49 states! (North Dakota awaits) and I have lived in seven, visited 43 countries, (many await)—many more mile markers. I recently moved—another mile marker. If I count right, I believe this was my 25th move as an adult. Twenty-five years ago, our family moved to Louisiana from (much to the chagrin of our children) San Diego, California.

There have been marriages, divorces and deaths, basically everything from the happiest of times to the hardest of times. But there is one consistency in every mile marker I have passed—God.

- Even when the storms rage so fierce—God is there.
- In the midst of the miracles of birth—God is there.
- In death, both physical and relational—God is there.
- In what seems hopeless leaving me feeling helpless—God is there.

Mile marker after mile marker, He has consistently been there even when I didn't feel His presence. There is such joy in my heart as I read back over this. The past year has been full of challenges for me. Struggling with two and three crises at a time has taken a toll on me, but God has been right there with me—as I rely on His wisdom, His presence and His love for me to shine through every tough conversation.

Looking forward, I can see the mile stones ahead but not the scenery. Like the fog limiting my view in this picture, I do not know what awaits, or how close the shore is, but I know God does.

> The continual presence of God is
> where my confidence lies.

My hope lies in my God. In every moment today and every moment to come, I will rise to meet the challenges of life and face them with confidence. I keep moving to the next milestone and the one after that and the next—until God decides that's enough and I move into eternity with Him. Keep moving as you pass yours too. Trust God to be with you. Even when you doubt, ask Him to show you where He is in the midst of illness, tragedy, loss, grief and anger.

TRY SOMETHING DIFFERENT

At some point, you realize you wake up every day to the same madness and every mile marker looks the same. Today, try something different. Stop and invite God into your chaos. When I began to recognize His presence, my life changed. It looked much different than anything I had anticipated. He accepted me. He saw the real me and loved me even more. His love is tender. He is kind. He is hope. He is love.

He has asked me to do things that take much courage as I release people, forgive them and look at Him instead of the chaos around me. But then looking back, I know how much He has forgiven me. And as my awareness of my sin becomes clearer, my view of forgiveness changes. Too often, we keep our personal sins at bay by letting the fog distort their presence. It is easier to focus on sin in the world and others all around us, but not so easy naming and facing our own.

Much courage is required to admit how sinful we are. Recognizing our sinful nature, acknowledging our need for our Creator's forgiveness and accepting it changes everything. His forgiveness brings clarity and a powerful desire to share that newfound hope with the world. God's love for us is the light that burns the fog off and lets the blue skies fill our vision.

Being forgiven makes space in my heart to love stronger, love more compassionately and to spread that love mile after mile as I travel through life.

I'm grateful I'm able to look back at the mile markers behind me. The presence of God is what stands out most to me. I see clearly where He showed up. I remember learning to let Him in when I rejected other relationships with all but a few. Today, I'm comforted that He will be with me every step of my life from this day forward. He has never asked me to travel these miles alone. He's not going to ask you to do that either. Here's to another 100,000 miles—mile marker by mile marker.

> *"I have fought the good fight, I have finished the race, I have kept the faith."* 2 Timothy 4:7 ESV

Lord, come close. When we can't even see the next mile marker, please come close. We remember the times You carried us through mile by mile. We want to honor You by sharing that hope with others around us who are searching for a way to rise above the helplessness. Let us be a willing vessel sharing Your hope. Let us walk together mile by mile with You. We love You, Lord. In Jesus' name. Amen.

John the Baptist's father was unable to speak from the day he laughed when his wife told him she was pregnant. At John's circumcision, his voice returned and he spoke this beautiful and tender message full of the hope of our future:

"He wants us to be holy and godly as long as we live. And you, my child, will be called a prophet of the Most High God. You will go ahead of the Lord to prepare the way for him. You will tell his people how they can be saved. You will tell them that their sins can be forgiven. All of that will happen because our God is tender and caring. His kindness will bring the rising sun to us from heaven. It will shine on those living in darkness and in the shadow of death. It will guide our feet on the path of peace."
Luke 1:75-79 NIrV

"He will wipe away every tear from their eyes. There will be no more death or sadness. There will be no more crying or pain. Things are no longer the way they used to be."
Revelation 21:4 NIrV

Glimpses & Reflections

1. Are you beginning to see the mile markers in your past that reveal God's presence in situations? List the first few that come to mind.

2. Think about forgiveness and how it connects to your ability to move on to the next mile marker. Write your thoughts about this.

3. How are you learning to be content and trust God when you can't see what lies ahead?

I've watched the older woman who lives at this house prepare the flower beds in the fall. She has someone who helps her plant the bulbs and then she waits. So do I. There is such a beautiful display of hope when the weather is still chilly and the colors appear.

Chapter 24
BEAUTY REST

"Flowers appear on the earth; the season of singing has come; the cooing of doves is heard in our land."
Song of Solomon 2:12 ESV

There is a beauty in resting that I never learned to appreciate until the past few years. Our winters in southern Louisiana are mild compared to the rest of the country. In twenty-five years, I remember single digit temperatures only a few times, and snow has fallen maybe a half-dozen times. However, our leaves fall, our grass dies after the first frost, and the rains fall. Some days, it's twenty degrees and a half day later the temperature is in the upper sixties. By mid-February, the Japanese magnolias are already blooming and I can already see buds on the fruit trees.

But experience has taught me, winter is not over. Year after year, the yo-yo of winter and spring wear us out. *Is it going to be "wing" this week or "sprinter"?* It can't even make up its mind. Winter. Spring. Winter. Spring. Winter. Then one day, spring will get stronger. More buds appear and this time they get to bloom. Tiny sprigs of green begin to appear in the yard. Birds sing with a renewed spirit. And my spirit begins to fill with optimism in the cycle of life we all participate in.

REST AND RENEWAL

Resting is over and nature does what God designed it to do. Babies appear in the nest. Little bunnies follow their mamas. Even the armadillos that live under my house come trotting across the yard with their four babies bopping along. Renewal. Rest. Renewal. Rest.

In this next series of scripture, it is clear the psalmist has experienced seasons coming and going.

> *"I'm feeling terrible—I couldn't feel worse! Get me on my feet again. You promised, remember? When I told my story, you responded; train me well in your deep wisdom. Help me understand these things inside and out so I can ponder your miracle-wonders. My sad life's dilapidated, a falling-down barn; build me up again by your Word. Barricade the road that goes Nowhere; grace me with your clear revelation. I choose the true road to Somewhere, I post your road signs at every curve and corner. I grasp and cling to whatever you*

tell me; God, don't let me down! I'll run the course you lay out for me if you'll just show me how." Psalm 119:25-32 MSG

This is a beautiful prayer we can easily identify with. Praying the very words of scripture when we can't begin to find our own is a deep level of worship.

> Observing God's creation at work has taught me that my life will not stay in one season forever either.

The years roll by with seasons of drought, floods, harvest, rest and renewal. Such a beautiful display of Him at work. Even when we feel He isn't near, we have to remember He is. We, too, can turn our faces toward the warmth of the sun and listen as our voices rise in praise for His presence.

I hope your seasons of rest renew you. I pray this next season of spring is ready to put forth many buds and begin preparing you for a bountiful harvest season in later months.

Father, thank You for giving us times of rest. I see You clearer when I am still and wait for You. I am grateful but I need help learning to be still. It is hard when I feel I have a checklist I need to be finishing. Help me know a list is not where I will find the close relationship I seek with You. Let me slow down and see the new leaves and the beautiful flowers that display Your presence here. We love You, Lord. In Jesus' name. Amen.

Glimpses & Reflections

1. Do you feel so rushed through life that you forget to look at the seasons around you?

2. What can you do to become more intentional in being still and resting?

3. Do you struggle to be still? Does that make you uncomfortable?

I will always remember the day I climbed into a boat and headed across this body of water, the Bay of Fonseca, toward the Pacific Ocean. The colors were breathtaking.

Chapter 25

TIDE'S OUT

"For the word of the Lord is upright, and all his work is done in faithfulness. He loves righteousness and justice; the earth is full of the steadfast love of the Lord. By the word of the Lord the heavens were made, and by the breath of his mouth all their host. He gathers the waters of the sea as a heap; he puts the deeps in storehouses. Let all the earth fear the Lord; let all the inhabitants of the world stand in awe of him!"
Psalm 33:4-8 ESV

The tide is out, a long way out. The patterns in the sand reflect the light above. The clouds hover over San Miguel, the active volcano in El Salvador. Honduras' mainland is to the right. Nicaragua is just off the screen to the left. We were crossing the Gulf of Fonseca in a small four-person boat piloted by a native. The island of Amapala was our destination for the day—a beautiful beach on the Pacific Ocean.

When I look back at my pictures, I wonder how I've been incredibly blessed to travel to the places I've been. I've seen so many different things and met so many different peoples in many different cultures. Yet, I'm always reminded of how similar we all are in certain ways. We all seek the water. We all seek the Light, but the foods we enjoy look different around the world. Our tongues speak different languages. I've learned it is our likenesses and our differences that bring a deep, rich look to this earth we all share.

Just as the sand in the shallows to the deep waters reaching to the mountains contribute to this beautiful scene, our lives are so much richer when we all come together, each contributing our share to the artist's palette. This view would have been pretty without the beach or even if the waters were not so many shades of blue. You might even take away the mountains and it would still be beautiful. God's creation is like that. Beauty is always waiting to be found.

> *"By awesome deeds you answer us with righteousness, O God of our salvation, the hope of all the ends of the earth and of the farthest seas; the one who by his strength established the mountains, being girded with might; who stills the roaring of the seas, the roaring of their waves, the tumult of the peoples, so that those who dwell at the ends of the earth are in awe at your signs. You make the going out of the morning and the evening to shout for joy." Psalm 65:5-8 ESV*

But once you begin adding in the layers created by the mountains, the waters and the beach, a breath-taking scene is created. God is like that. He isn't a one-dimensional God. He is a triple layered artist a hundred times over as He creates a world waiting for us to explore.

DIFFERENT NATIONS BUT ONE HEART

Cultures, foods and beautiful people create a scene we need to seek. I have sat with women in many communities in Honduras. Meals have been shared in the villages we visited in India. I have worshipped with sisters, speaking encouragement into their lives while sitting next to a translator. I have visited women in Cairo who teach women skills that will change their lives because they can now generate income by sewing and quilting, or weaving co-ops in Lombok, an island in Indonesia.

We spent several days in northern Jordan on the Syrian border, with refugees learning to knit. Even though the hands of all these women were busy doing different tasks, our hearts all connected through the bond we share as women—women who love their children and want to provide for their families.

We need to see the beauty in all people and their lives that make this world look more like the world God intended when He created us. We are the ones who look at our inner circles and declare what the rest of the world is supposed to look like. Let's stop that. Let's love like our Creator created us to.

> Let's go higher than the flat view we have of the world to see His creation awaiting us.

> *"Steadfast love and faithfulness meet; righteousness and peace kiss each other. Faithfulness springs up from the ground, and righteousness looks down from the sky." Psalm 85:10-11 ESV*

Like His love, let's strive for ours to endure for the rest of our lives as we love our best into the people around us and into the generations to come.

> *"For the Lord is a great God, and a great King above all gods. In his hand are the depths of the earth; the heights of the mountains are his also. The sea is his, for he made it, and his hands formed the dry land. O come let us worship and bow down; let us kneel before the Lord, our Maker!" Psalm 95:3-6 ESV*

> *"Give thanks to the Lord, for he is good, for his steadfast love endures forever. Give thanks to the God of gods, for his steadfast love endures forever. Give thanks to the Lord of lords, for his steadfast love endures forever; to him who alone does great wonders, for his steadfast love endures forever; to him who by*

understanding made the heavens, for his steadfast love endures forever; to him who spread out the earth above the waters, for his steadfast love endures forever; to him who made the great lights, for his steadfast love endures forever; the sun to rule over the day, for his steadfast love endures forever; the moon and stars to rule over the night, for his steadfast love endures forever." Psalm 136:1-9 ESV

> Father, thank You for creating each of us with such a unique character. You have given us our own gifts to use so Your love will be reflected into the world. You love so well. May we each become the best possible as we serve You to the end of our days. In Jesus' name. Amen.

Understanding the love of God allows our hearts to trust Him.

"Dear children, don't just talk about love. Put your love into action. Then it will truly be love. That's how we know that we hold to the truth. And that's how we put our hearts at rest, knowing that God is watching. Our hearts may judge us. But God is greater than our hearts. He knows everything."
1 John 3:18-20 NIrV

"We love because he loved us first. Anyone who says he loves God but in fact hates his brother or sister is a liar. He doesn't love his brother or sister, whom he has seen. So he can't love God, whom he has not seen. Here is the command God has given us. Anyone who loves God must also love his brothers and sisters."
1 John 4:19-21 NIrV

Glimpses & Reflections

1. How dimensional do you consider your life to be?

2. How do you enjoy all the differences seen in others?

3. Write your favorite scripture referring to the praise of the world and creation we live in.

This door is on a home in an impoverished community in Tegucigalpa, Honduras.

Chapter 26
GOD IS LOVE

I feel overcome with sadness. How, Lord? How is this possible that such hatred can fill a human and that this hatred exists all over the world? How is it possible we live in our world where school shootings, mass shootings, car bombings and other wretched events are reported daily and with each occurrence becomes more normal to the world? The more I travel and engage in conversations with people in other parts of the world, the clearer view I have of how dark the evil is in our world.

Between sex trafficking and genocide reports, entire villages disappearing, the evil is growing deeper and darker all around us. I have heard stories of men attending auctions deep in the deserts to buy young children to satisfy their despicable desires. I have talked to parents in remote villages afraid to send their children to school because several from their community have been abducted, their body parts being sold on the black market.

How many of us (my hand raised here) are teetering on the brink of allowing that hatred to take up residency in our own hearts? We can hate the evil, crime and oppression, but what do we do when our response is hatred-based? Do we become as wrong as the offender in the crime we protest? How do we prevent ourselves from becoming the very thing we hate?

This is my challenge—every day. How do we raise our children and grandchildren to be different and live in a world of hate? Not as haters but as peacemakers? History teaches us that humanity is wicked. Only when we turn to the history recorded in Scripture do we see any glimmer of hope. We see how God came in, intervened and peace returned, albeit, until man returned to his old nature. But thankfully, God continues teaching us how to live today by assuring us the battle and the victory belong to us because we belong to Him.

> *"For the Lord your God is he who goes with you to fight for you against your enemies, to give you the victory." Deuteronomy 20:4 ESV*
>
> *"But thanks be to God! He gives us the victory through our Lord Jesus Christ." 1 Corinthians 15:57 NIV*

WE DO NOT FIGHT ALONE

We know the enemies we face are evil, but we do not fight them alone. God is fully aware of them and gives us this peace. He even tells us to be thankful.

> *"Let the peace that Christ gives rule in your hearts. As parts of one body, you were appointed to live in peace. And be thankful." Colossians 3:15 NIRV*

It's really hard to feel the peace Paul talks about here. Life events consistently try to rob us of any peace. If we focus on all the injustice in the world, we can be filled with anger. Only when we focus on the words in scriptures like this are we able to move beyond horror and step into peace.

> *"My dear brothers, take note of this: Everyone should be quick to listen, slow to speak and slow to become angry, for man's anger does not bring about the righteous life that God desires. Therefore, get rid of all moral filth and the evil that is so prevalent and humbly accept the word planted in you, which can save you. Do not merely listen to the word, and so deceive yourselves. Do what it says. Anyone who listens to the word but does not do what it says is like a man who looks at his face in a mirror and, after looking at himself, goes away and immediately forgets what he looks like. But the man who looks intently into the perfect law that gives freedom, and continues to do this, not forgetting what he has*

heard, but doing it—he will be blessed in what he does." James 2:19-25 NIV84

Only when I pray like this am I able to remove the hatred of my flesh and replace it with what Jesus teaches. We gain forgiveness, repentance, a desire to be close to Him, love and finally a peace that truly passes all understanding as the Holy Spirit becomes part of who we are.

In Jesus, we are transformed.

When we follow His commands and obey His instruction, we can rise out of the hopeless turmoil and hatred thriving in humanity. Only then will we find protection from the hatred swirling around us. Only then will we be able to focus on making a difference in this world. Only then will we be able to make wise decisions that will keep our hearts focused on being peace makers.

Will we be able to change everyone in the world? No, we are not God. It is His peace in us that changes the community we live in because it moves us beyond ourselves. That is where our thankful hearts can rest.

> *"So get rid of every kind of evil. Stop telling lies. Don't pretend to be something you are not. Stop wanting what others have. Don't speak against each other. Like babies that were just born, you should long for the*

pure milk of God's word. It will help you grow up as believers. You can do it now that you have tasted how good the Lord is." 1 Peter 2:1-5 NIRV

We have been given the gift of prayer and can pray for the world. We can spread hope and peace with every errand we run, every conversation we have, every person who cuts us off on the highway, every person who cuts in line or shares every conversation at work.

We can rest now—knowing it is not by our power but by the power of God's presence in our lives that we can reject helplessness and share the hopefulness and thankfulness He brings us.

"Run away from infantile indulgence. Run after mature righteousness—faith, love, peace—joining those who are in honest and serious prayer before God. Refuse to get involved in inane discussions; they always end up in fights. God's servant must not be argumentative, but a gentle listener and a teacher who keeps cool, working firmly but patiently with those who refuse to obey." 2 Timothy 2:23-25 MSG

Lord, help us focus on You in these times of hopelessness. Fill us with Your hope and peace. Give us the wisdom we need to know when to speak and when to be silent. In Jesus' name. Amen.

Glimpses & Reflections

1. How can we overcome the level of hatred that has become almost "normal" in today's society?

2. How do you typically respond when you find yourself embroiled in a conversation turning divisive?

3. Write a prayer asking God to help you know how to respond?

My personal workspace is special these days. I have an office and a desk but I prefer sitting by the window in my dining room or on my porch watching the world go by. Many times, you can find me at our camp in the woods. The light in both places inspires me and keeps me connected to God and this work I'm fully committed to.

Chapter 27
FINISHING

This is my current work space and I love it. This is where I sit, working on finishing the final product. I noticed this quirk in my personality that tries to keep me from finishing certain writing projects. This is strange because I love to write and it's always been easy for me. However, the editing, rewriting and feelings of "doing it all over again" have been the easy excuses for me to push back and begin working on a new project.

Really, it's fear. It's not so much putting in the hard work it takes to finish a book and bringing it to print that has terrified me, but rather revealing that part of me to the world. I'm afraid of what someone might think or say negatively about it. Many writers compare getting a book out to the birthing process. I happen to think that's a perfect analogy.

I had to learn a new way of thinking. I have found myself in conversations lately and hear my words, "but, God". I can face the biggest mountain and wonder how in the world this mountain that is too big to go around and too tall to climb over, can possibly be conquered, "but, God."

> *"Jesus looked at them and said, 'With man, that is impossible. But with God, all things are possible.'" Matthew 19:26 NIRV*

Over and over again in my story, the impossible looms ahead. Scary and lonely, it created great doubt in me. "But, God." God showed up through His Word. It is alive and speaks exactly what I need to hear at the perfect time. Even when it is one of the most familiar to me, reading it one more time gives fresh insight to the mountain I'm facing at the time.

> *"But God shows his love for us in that while we were still sinners, Christ died for us." Romans 5:8 ESV*

This is where I learned to trust and believe. It is in those "but, God" moments that I feel a balance I had never known. God does that for us. He is near and I'm understanding how He has been preparing me for this time for over six decades. Sometimes, I laugh at how slow a learner I can be, "but, God"—His timing is perfect, and I rest in that.

> "But God raised him from the dead. He set him free from the suffering of death. It wasn't possible for death to keep its hold on Jesus." Acts 2:24 NIRV

God sent Jesus to earth knowing His plan. Jesus knew what the next years of His life would require of Him. He never waned from the plan of bringing the message of forgiveness and redemption to the world. Even when the hard days came, He stayed faithful to His Father's plan.

> "Later Jesus said, 'I am thirsty.' He knew that everything was now finished. He knew that what Scripture said must come true. A jar of wine vinegar was there. So they soaked a sponge in it. They put the sponge on a stem of the hyssop plant. Then they lifted it up to Jesus' lips. After Jesus drank he said, 'It is finished'. Then he bowed his head and died." John 19:28-30 NIRV

I want to finish the work God has given me.

He has given us everything we need to be faithful to the eternal cause. He created each of us with the exact, unique formula to faithfully serve Him. Together, we complete the beautiful plan He has. Jesus did every part of what God asked of Him. He fulfilled every prophecy from the Old Testament. I pray you and I will be willing to do the same.

Lord, Thank You for Your patience with us. Thank You for filling us up when we are exhausted and giving us glimpses of Your presence day by day. We thank You for new relationships in our community and are grateful for old friends as well. Use us in this story to Your glory! In Jesus' name. Amen.

Glimpses & Reflections

1. When have you heard yourself say, "but, God"? Write down the details.

2. Do you feel committed to completing a task you have been putting off because of fear? Write about it.

3. Write a prayer asking God to give you clarity and courage to be able to complete this task.

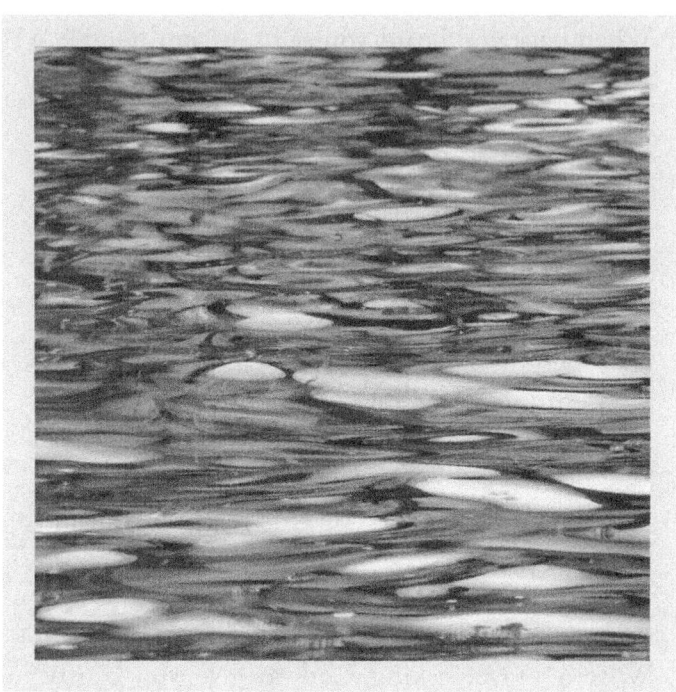

This shot of the water at the lake one lazy afternoon is not edited. I can tell it was cloudy because I see the white of the clouds reflected. Raindrops were beginning to fall. You can see their effect on the water. Look closer and you will see several places where the boat is reflected as well.

Chapter 28
RHYTHMS AND REFLECTIONS

Light is magnetic, both physically and spiritually, drawing me in a rhythm like the one on the shore of a lake or a beach of the ocean. Light reflects off certain surfaces. The moon wouldn't be visible if it didn't reflect the sun. Without light, I would see nothing in the mirror. Inner reflection shows me where I am. When I turn my focus inward, I see clues to my current self and what is going on not just around me but in me. I see circumstances I've faced and how I have engaged with them.

When my mom passed, questions clouded my horizon. I didn't know how to go on without her. We had been through so much together. Our bond deepened after Dad's death and my divorce. We talked about regrets and how to move forward. Mom slowly worked through her anger at Dad for getting Alzheimer's (a common emotion of the caregivers in that situation). Fear and the unknown of the future clouded my reflections.

During all those times, Mom and I were looking around at the surface. Only when we began to look deeper into our relationships with God were we able to see a shift in our outlook. We would sit in the living room at night and I would read her something I had written or something I was reading and we would talk about it, both laughing and crying, sometimes simultaneously. I learned more about my mom in those few years than I had in all my life.

STAYING CONNECTED

The closer I stay connected to God through prayer and study of His Word, the clearer the reflection I see of Him in me and the steadier the rhythm moving me closer to Him. Clearly, I was beginning to rise out of the helplessness I had been fixated on.

Spaces of calm where I can sit in peace and see clearly are only seasons. Basking in the light of the sun when it shines teaches me to appreciate those moments. Life has taught me there will always be another season coming. Even in the difficult seasons I remember, no one season lasts forever. While climbing the mountain, no view stays the same. The higher we go, the more we see. However, the level roads and the ones requiring mountain climbing gear all require participation from me. I must turn to God on a deeper level daily

> "The Lord is near to all who call on him, to all who call on him in truth." Psalm 145:18 ESV

I cannot always see an undistorted reflection but I can always count on God's presence in those times. The one part I keep in mind is how the light changes the reflection. When I choose the light of Christ, it changes everything. My faith deepens and my response changes. Sometimes faith looks like an elevator, an escalator or a hiking trail on a mountain. All are designed to raise us to a new level.

Let's sing and rejoice in the beauty of the newness God showers us with. Faith is like this. Faith is alive. It flourishes when we actively engage and nurture it through prayer and study of God's Word.

> God designed us to engage our faith, put our confidence in Him, and allow Him to carry us through.

These words below are such beautiful reminders of His presence in our lives.

> "But God chose you to be his people. You are royal priests. You are a holy nation. You are a people who belong to God. All of this is so that you can sing

his praises. He brought you out of darkness into his wonderful light. Once you were not a people. But now you are the people of God. Once you had not received mercy. But now you have received mercy." 1 Peter 2:9-10 NIRV

> Lord, come close. Bring us the clarity we need to see You in ways that will make our paths clear. Define our purpose and lead us. Reflections can confuse us many times distorting the way we should live. Other times we see You in our reflections. Thank You for sending Jesus to die for our sins. We love You, Lord. In Jesus' name. Amen.

Glimpses & Reflections

1. How do you see yourself releasing the old you and grabbing hold of a new you in your relationship with God? Be sure to write down the joys you are experiencing.

2. How do you engage your faith?

3. What do the reflections of your surroundings reveal? Are you moving closer or further away from Him?

As the day ends and the night moves in, the light fades. In the darkness, our fears often come to life. We sense them near. Their voice overpowers us. When we read what Jesus has to say about fear, we learn He is fully aware of our struggles. His words reassure us He wants us to rest fearlessly in His presence.

Chapter 29
FEAR NOT

Fear is not to be underestimated. Ever. It is a powerful influencer in our lives. A huge part of my emotional state through the process of a divorce was deeply rooted in fear. I feared loss, rejection, disagreements, being less than, left out, and different. Basically, the unknown. I carried shame, deep, bone-chilling shame. Everything I had *been* taught, *had* taught and believed was destroyed as I checked "D" for marital status. This was never supposed to be part of my life.

Every relationship I had was changed. Even with my adult children. We were no longer a family unit. We stood divided and had no clue how to move forward. Almost every decision I made was rooted in fear and guilt. I blamed myself for not being able to keep our family together. I saw the pain in their eyes when they forgot and mentioned their dad and saw their pain reflected in my eyes.

All of this was rooted in fear, and Jesus knew we would face it often. His words here assure us we don't need to be afraid.

> "But he said to them, 'It is I; do not be afraid.'" John 6:20 ESV

There was a time when that old saying, "Insanity is when you wake up every day, do the same thing over and over expecting a different outcome" played out in my life one time too many. I knew I had to change and that change began with addressing my fears. My fear of trusting anyone ever again was my biggest hurdle.

> "Lord, those who know you will trust in you. You have never deserted those who look to you." Psalm 9:10 NIRV

> "When I'm afraid, I will trust in you. I trust in God. I praise his word. I trust in God. I will not be afraid. What can people do to me?" Psalm 53:3-4 NIRV

When I slowly realized by testing the waters of all the church lessons I carried in my memories, I discovered God meant it when He told me He loved me with His perfect love. Perfection is not possible for me. I had to release that struggle. Read and ponder this verse again, and again.

> "There is no fear in love; but perfect love casts out fear, because fear involves punishment, and the one who

fears is not perfected in love. We love, because He first loved us." 1 John 4:18-19 NIRV

Overcome fear by walking with Jesus. We can't overcome fears until we face them.

"Have I not commanded you? Be strong and courageous. Do not be frightened, and do not be dismayed, for the Lord your God is with you wherever you go." Joshua 1:9 ESV

Live free. Live brave. Live courageously. Believing in God's love for us changes everything. Slowly our eyes begin to rise to the heavens as we look around at the creation we see and read the words these God-inspired writers recorded for us. His Words are alive. Words that continue to apply to our lives today. Our focus is on the Light instead of the darkness trying its best to swallow us. Like the sun rises bringing light, we rise bringing the Light of Jesus in us to the world.

"This is how we know we're living steadily and deeply in him, and he in us: He's given us life from his life, from his very own Spirit. Also, we've seen for ourselves and continue to state openly that the Father sent his Son as Savior of the world. Everyone who confesses that Jesus is God's Son participates continuously in an intimate relationship with God. We know it so well, we've embraced it heart and soul, this love that comes from God." 1 John 4:13-16 MSG

Scripture is everything to me. It has helped me through some of the darkest times. In each chapter I have included some of my favorites for you to meditate on. Be encouraged as you rise from the valleys through the middle and on to the mountaintops

> "The Lord is my light and my salvation; whom shall I fear? The Lord is the stronghold of my life; of whom shall I be afraid? When evildoers assail me to eat up my flesh, my adversaries and foes, it is they who stumble and fall. Though an army encamp against me, my heart shall not fear; though war arise against me, yet I will be confident.

> "One thing have I asked of the Lord, that will I seek after: that I may dwell in the house of the Lord all the days of my life, to gaze upon the beauty of the Lord and to inquire in his temple. For he will hide me in his shelter in the day of trouble; he will conceal me under the cover of his tent; he will lift me high upon a rock.

> "And now my head shall be lifted up above my enemies all around me, and I will offer in his tent sacrifices with shouts of joy; I will sing and make melody to the Lord. Hear, O Lord, when I cry aloud; be gracious to me and answer me! You have said, 'Seek my face.' My heart says to you, 'Your face, Lord, do I seek.' Hide not your face from me. Turn not your servant away in

anger, O you who have been my help. Cast me not off; forsake me not, O God of my salvation!

"For my father and my mother have forsaken me, but the Lord will take me in. Teach me your way, O Lord, and lead me on a level path because of my enemies. Give me not up to the will of my adversaries; for false witnesses have risen against me, and they breathe out violence.

"I believe that I shall look upon the goodness of the Lord in the land of the living! Wait for the Lord; be strong, and let your heart take courage; wait for the Lord!" Psalm 27 ESV

> Lord, thank You for giving us Your Word. It sustains and lifts us up. Thank You for creating us with hearts that can know and experience the depth of Your love. In Jesus' name. Amen.

Paul as a prisoner, writes this letter to the Ephesians. This excerpt is his prayer for them and for us.

"I bow in prayer to the Father because of my work among you. From the Father his whole family in heaven and on earth gets its name. I pray that he will use his glorious riches to make you strong. May his Holy Spirit give you his power deep down inside you. Then Christ will live in your hearts because you believe in him. And I pray that your love will have deep roots. I pray that it will have a strong foundation. May you have power with all God's people to understand Christ's love.

"May you know how wide and long and high and deep it is. And may you know his love, even though it can't be known completely. Then you will be filled with everything God has for you. God is able to do far more than we could ever ask for or imagine. He does everything by his power that is working in us. Give him glory in the church and in Christ Jesus. Give him glory through all time and for ever and ever. Amen."
Ephesians 3:14-21 NIrV

Glimpses & Reflections

1. What is your favorite scripture and why?

2. What is a fear you want to overcome?

3. Write a prayer asking God to help you overcome that fear and develop a deeper relationship with Him.

I wish you had been standing with me the day I took this picture on the shores of the Sea of Galilee. These stones lay on the beach as remnants of an old building that used to stand nearby. This is supposedly the site where Jesus prepared fish for the disciples as they returned early one morning from fishing all night.

Chapter 30
LOVE LIKE HIM

"A new commandment I give to you, that you love one another, even as I have loved you, that you also love one another. By this all men will know that you are My disciples, if you have love for one another."
John 13:34-35 NASB95

One morning, a sweet laboratory technician and I were talking about how wise her daughter and my then fifteen-year-old granddaughter were. We marveled at their ability to know everything, wishing we were that wise at that age (chuckle, chuckle). As an "older" woman, I marvel that I have made it this far in life and still don't know much. I've always wanted to be that wise grandmother with sage advice. But I don't give up. I learn every day.

My grandchildren span over eighteen years. I wish I could tell all of them how important love is. I want them to understand what a gift God gave us when He designed our hearts to love. I want them to understand love is not only about the person you love but also about who loves you. It's about loving God and loving ourselves as the person God created us to be.

Have you ever:
- Walked the ocean beach?
- Held a newborn baby?
- Watched a butterfly emerge from its cocoon?

We marvel at these and other amazing things God created around us, but what do we see when we look in the mirror? Do we stand in awe of the person we see reflecting God's creation? We need to stop the doubt, the self-loathing and the voice of negativity we hear critiquing the image in the mirror. Maybe you go through times when you don't even want to look in the mirror? There have been times when I couldn't even look myself in the eye.

My words of wisdom would be:

> Courageously loving yourself as a creation of our Father God will bring every other aspect of love into focus.

FOCUS ON WHOSE YOU ARE

Never entertain the thought of a self-serving love being sufficient or real. Only make room for a God-serving love to take root in you. There may be seasons when you feel deeply loved and there may be seasons when you don't. Never accept less than what God has planned for you in a relationship. The best is when both of you are focused on God. Keep your eyes on Him. Count on Him and reject anything that does not have actions to back it up.

Stay out of relationship with anyone that doesn't love God like you do. There may be times you will watch the world celebrate Valentine's Day—alone. You will look around and feel unlovable. Ask me how I know. Do not accept or believe this lie. You are incredibly lovable and never alone. Rise above every message that would rob you of God's plan for you. Know that true love begins with your relationship with God. Don't settle for anything less than the best God has for you.

It's not about who you are, but whose. You are a beloved child of the King of kings, the Father of all creation, the Savior who died for your sins, the Holy Spirit who lives in you and you are loved.

> *"The LORD your God is in your midst, a mighty one who will save; he will rejoice over you with gladness; he will quiet you by his love; he will exult over you with loud singing." Zephaniah 3:17 ESV*

> Lord, come close and help me remember the depth of Your love for me. Remove the idea that I am unlovable. Help me, Lord. Fill me with Your presence. Show me the way past these lies. Lift me up. In Jesus' name. Amen.

Glimpses & Reflections

1. Describe a time when you felt "less than".

2. Find a scripture that explains how much God loves you. Write it down and memorize it.

3. Write a prayer asking God to help you understand His love and watch how this is going to change your life.

The streets of Brooklyn host an amazing array of graffiti. Many of them beautiful displays of the artist's talents in clear, concise composition. This one, however, intrigued me. It appears to be layer upon layer of evidence of many artists over many years. No one clear message, but rather a jumbled collection of thoughts.

Chapter 31
NAME THAT FUNK

My goal is to use every part of my testimony for God in me and around me and to share Him with the world. The best thing about my testimony is that all my past sins are forgiven and I am free. Everything is erased and I am standing in the presence of God, fully forgiven and blessed and richly empowered to live my best life. He changes everything. How can I be quiet about that?

> *"Sing your songs to Zion-dwelling God, tell his stories to everyone you meet" Psalm 9:11 MSG*

Yet, some days it feels like a wet blanket coming down over me again from oppositional events. For example, this week I had two days to devote to a project. Out of nowhere, a tooth broke which meant a three-hour dentist appointment. Then, a strange lump appeared creating havoc with my schedule. Three appointments, an ultrasound, waiting,

waiting and waiting for the doctor to call only to find out all reports point to a benign tumor.

Moving past that, it was my daughter's birthday. Memories flood my being on these special days. Times shared with my husband, her actual birth day, and having a precious baby girl join our world affect my inner emotions. Good memories. And there I sat. I continued reading scripture, praying and surrounding myself with faithful friends. My music played in the background as dogs and cat napped, cars passed on the street outside and to top it off, it was raining.

From nowhere came the thought, *Name that funk, Janet. Name it.*

Through all these pieces of me I just shared with you, I can see the thread running through them—memories. Memories bring back the joy of days gone by, but they also carry the reminder of loss. Loss of our family unit, loss of trust, loss of growing old together and loss of serving together round out the pile of pieces. Loss of going through challenges with someone by my side. This isn't the first time I've sat among these pieces and it probably won't be the last, either.

Funk, meet Loss.

WHERE I FIND PEACE

The years since hurricane Katrina have taught me to find peace in God's Word. The Bible has become my retreat. Experiences I never saw coming led me into the pages of the Bible in a whole new way.

My enthusiasm for sharing my personal testimony regularly is to reach a hand out to others stranded in that same no man's land I experienced. That was the place where we either sink deeper into despair or we turn to the truth in God's Word. God wrote my testimony for me. He uses it to empower me and those I share it with to rise out of the funk. These stories remind me of His presence in my life in the good and the bad. It is there He became my God of all things. He holds His hand out to me and lifts me out from among the rubble to rise up to Him. God's hand waits for you as well.

May my testimony be a blessing to you, my struggles point you to a deeper relationship with God and show how God wrote my testimony and yours. Whoever said there will be no testimony without a test knew what they were talking about. May you seek God as yours is being written. God is great!

> *(God is speaking) "I am honored all over the world. And there are people who know how to worship me all over the world, who honor me by bringing their best*

to me. They're saying it everywhere: 'God is greater, this God-of-the-Angel-Armies.'" Malachi 1:11 MSG

> Lord, thank You for always being with us even in the chaos and funk. Forgive us when we forget how much You love us. Heal us in our broken places. Restore us to serve You best. Ease the pain of loss. Transform us into the best version of us You have designed us to be. We love You, Lord. Thank You for listening. In Jesus' name. Amen.

Glimpses & Reflections

1. Can you see God's thread woven through your testimony? Name some specific times and details.

2. When you reflect on some of the hard times from your past, are you able to see Him now that you are further out from the situation?

3. What can you do to bring your focus back on God when you are in the middle of a funk?

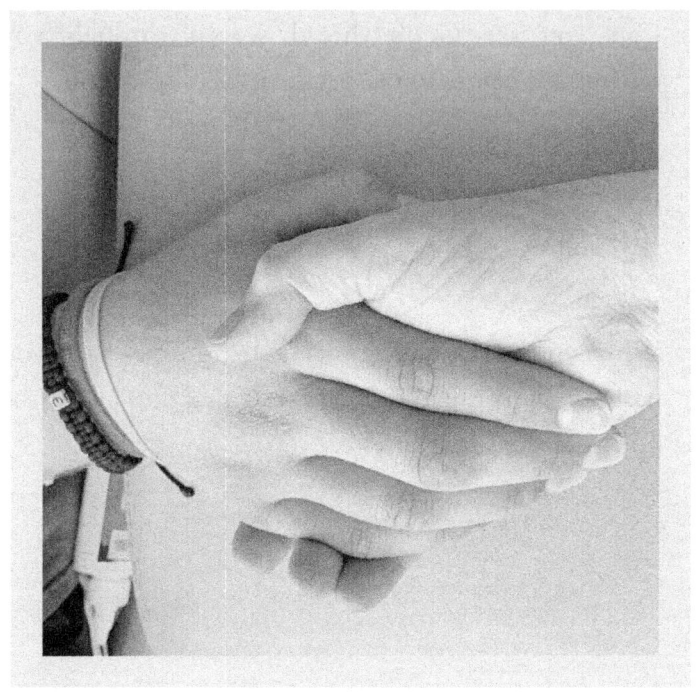

Since that day twelve years ago Christian and I have spent a lot of time together. It amazes me the number of times I get to teach him something. It's even sweeter to me that he listens. I pray for those moments and I pray that my ear will always be tuned in to hear the subtle questions in every conversation.

Chapter 32

WHAT I LEARNED FROM A CAN OF TUNA...AND MY GRANDSON

For us and many others, the kitchen is the center of our family's life together. It is a warm and special place to me. I designed our kitchen to be welcoming and family-friendly. When people come in, they pull up a bar stool to the island and enjoy some of the most memorable and meaningful conversations.

One sunny afternoon, I was hanging out with my six-year-old grandson, Christian, and four-year-old sister, Emma, as they planted flowers. Time passed quickly while we were working outside and we soon realized we needed some lunch. So, we went into the kitchen and began preparing.

We had decided we would have tuna salad for lunch. Christian was helping me by peeling and chopping the eggs. Next, I picked up a can of tuna and asked him if he knew how to open it. He looked up at me with his brilliant, blue Italian eyes and what he said made my heart skip a beat. I think it actually stopped, now that I think about it.

He looked at me with the most innocent eyes and whispered, "No, Nana, but can you teach me?" He was afraid if he spoke too loudly, his self-appointed rule-keeper and enforcer, Emma, would hear him and tell him he wasn't allowed to use a can opener. When I regained my composure, I whispered to him, "Of course, I will teach you."

We went through the mechanics of operating a manual can opener and he proceeded to open both cans. He was so pleased with himself! He had learned something he didn't know he was capable of learning. After he had completed his task, he stood a little taller next to me.

It made me ask myself:

- *When was the last time I put myself on the line in such an honest and pure way asking God to teach me something I felt I was incapable of learning?*
- *How often do I approach Him with that unfiltered, an all-boundaries-removed and focused plea?*

- *When was the last time I laid all of me aside and came before Him sincerely, with all the Janet-baggage out of the way?*

I know I mundanely ask Him for help every day. I'm not talking about that. I want to come before my Father with that same innocence as Christian showed, like Moses approached the burning bush. I desire that boldness, that courage—things I know come only from being forgiven of my sins that separate me from that kind of close relationship with God, my Father. Christian was not afraid to look me straight in the eyes and ask for help.

- Am I capable of doing that with God?
- Is it possible for us to come to a place where we can be that honest with God?
- Do you struggle with this as heavily as I do?

I know what it was like to have Christian trust me to answer his question and teach him what he wanted to know. I imagine it makes God feel the same way when I ask Him to teach me. I want to become more like Moses as he stood before God on the mountain in the wilderness in Exodus.

> *"If you are pleased with me, teach me your ways so I may know you and continue to find favor with you."*
> *Exodus 33:13 NIV84*

Perhaps you, like Christian and I, have feared that all the rule-followers might shout, "You can't talk to God like that!" Maybe it starts out with whispering to God. He will be there waiting to hear our pleas. This step of courage is between each of us and God. Are you ready to remove the barriers that have grown around you and making you feel separated from this kind of relationship with Him? I want to stand on that holy ground of confidence in my relationship with Him and know that He is MY God and I am worthy of Him teaching me what He needs me to know.

My prayer is that this will encourage you to seek a deeper and closer walk with God.

- How deep can you go?
- What is it going to take to move you closer to Him?
- Don't you desire to stand a little taller?

By listening carefully to my grandson, I learned a lesson I didn't realize I needed so desperately. The years ahead were going to be hard. Changing how I approached God was the hinge that would open new doors in my relationship with Him. While I was playing the role of teacher, my six-year-old was actually teaching me. Our children and grandchildren are precious treasures in so many ways. Listen to them and pay attention. You will be amazed.

I'm continually learning to observe how God comes alongside me when I ask, and teaches me how to live the life He has planned for me as I experience His "yes". In those moments, I have the deepest sense of joy. I really had no idea how beautiful His joy plays out in my life. Living joyfully changes the outcome of every difficult road. I pray you too will soon experience this joy.

> Lord, thank You for filling our lives with people who teach us to ask the honest questions. Teach us to come before You as little children with faith that crosses the barriers we hide behind. Help us as we come closer to You. Hear our hearts. Fill our lives with deep and joy-filled relationship with You. Amen.

Here, Moses is talking to the Israelites. What a comfort to us all to have unrestricted access to God.

"What I'm commanding you today is not too hard for you. It isn't beyond your reach. It isn't up in heaven. So you don't have to ask, 'Who will go up into heaven to get it? Who will announce it to us so we can obey it?' And it isn't beyond the ocean. So you don't have to ask, 'Who will go across the ocean to get it? Who will announce it to us so we can obey it?' No, the message isn't far away at all. In fact, it's really near you. It's in your mouth and in your heart so that you can obey it."
Deuteronomy 30:11-14 NIrV

Glimpses & Reflections

1. What is the first question you want to ask God?

2. What do you deeply desire to learn about living life with God? Identify the moments you experience the godly joy.

3. Find a scripture that relates to this desire. Forgiveness, dealing with anxiety, raising children, etc.

Sun rising or setting, this open sky over Lake Ponchartrain near New Orleans, Louisiana, creates a beautiful palette as God displays His presence through His creation and reminds me often how my own journey rises and falls. Yet with God, the circle is completed.

Chapter 33

IT IS WELL

Scripture is everything to me. It has helped me through some of the darkest times. In each chapter I have included some of my favorites for you to meditate on. Be encouraged as you rise.

"It is Well" was written in 1873 by Horatio G. Stafford. At that time, his wife and four daughters were on a transatlantic journey to Europe. Their ship was struck by another vessel and sunk. All four daughters drowned. His wife was rescued. She was in Europe. Her telegram to him read "Saved alone. What shall I do . . ."

He headed to Europe to her. As their ship passed over the place where his daughters had died, the captain came to him—the waters three miles deep. Horatio wrote to his wife, "But I do not think of our dear ones there. They are safe . . . dear lambs."

His inspiration for this song is found here.

> "Beloved, I pray that all may go well with you and that you may be in good health, as it goes well with your soul." 3 John 1:2 ESV

Awareness of my soul status heightens as the chaos in the world around me is relentless. Life continues to present struggle after struggle. Only when I retreat into the inner most parts of me does my awareness of God's connection to and His presence in my soul bring any relief to the chaos. It is then the storms begin to calm. Having a solid connection to God stabilizes my soul.

This short parable of Jesus in Matthew 8 calms not just the storms around me but the storms within me as well. My faith in Him continues to grow as I see the evidence of His work not just around me, but within.

I cry out to Him in faith—a faith that is sometimes wobbling in the wake of life storms. Even in my small faith, His love for me (and you) is so great that He will command the winds of chaos that wreak havoc and the waves of fear that threaten to pull me (and you) under forever, to "be still."

No matter how hard I attempt to create "happy" around me with beautiful places, good food, great company, and the best of all things, if my soul is lacking, the joy never connects. It gets stuck somewhere between "deep down in" and "the light in my eyes."

The struggle is not always calmed around me, but I can always count on His voice to calm the storm within me and ease the fear that echoes the voice of the enemy. I have stood in storms so fierce that I was certain drowning was inevitable.

> It was impossible to believe God would hear my cries for help over the pounding of the waves, but . . . He did.

"And when he got into the boat, his disciples followed him. And behold, there arose a great storm on the sea, so that the boat was being swamped by the waves; but he was asleep. And they went and woke him, saying, 'Save us, Lord; we are perishing.' And he said to them, 'Why are you afraid, O you of little faith?' Then he rose and rebuked the winds and the sea, and there was a great calm. And the men marveled, saying, 'What sort of man is this, that even winds and sea obey him?'"
Matthew 8:23-27 ESV

The storm on the sea around the disciples and the storm of fear within them were both stilled. It is with great peace deep in my soul that no matter the storms on the horizon of my life, I confidently know my God is there where even the winds and the waves obey Him.

> Father, we come humbly before You. We ask for a healing from doubt and a release from the fears that keep us from walking closer with You. Even as we watch storms appear on the horizon, please give us the peace that passes understanding, help us to remember Your promises to always be near and that our experiences from the past confirm Your presence is always with us. Forgive us when we struggle; thank You for the grace and redemption You shower us with. We love You, Lord. We praise You in our storms, past, present, and yet to come. In Jesus' name. Amen.

Following are the original lyrics to the song we love. This man, who endured such tragedy, wrote a song giving praise to God in his circumstances and His presence in his life. I believe our song of praise can join in the chorus of love, as we lift our voices to the heavens in awe and worship of our heavenly King. May it be well with our souls.

It Is Well
By Horatio G. Stafford

When peace like a river, attendeth my way,
When sorrows like sea billows roll;
Whatever my lot, Thou hast taught me to know,
It is well, it is well, with my soul.

It is well,
With my soul,
It is well, it is well with my soul.

Though Satan should buffet, though trials should come,
Let this blest assurance control,
That Christ has regarded my helpless estate,
And hath shed His own blood for my soul.

My sin, of, the bliss of this glorious thought!
My sin, not in part but the whole
Is nailed to the cross and I bear it no more,

Praise the Lord, praise the Lord, O my soul!

For me, be it Christ, be it Christ hence to live;
If Jordan above me shall roll,
No pang shall be mine, for in death as in life,
Thou wilt whisper Thy peace to my soul.

But Lord, 'tis for Thee, for Thy coming we wait,

The sky, not the grave, is our goal;
Oh, trump of the angel! Oh, voice of the Lord!
Blessed hope, blessed rest of my soul.

And Lord, haste the day when the faith shall be sight.
The clouds be rolled back as a scroll;
The trump shall resound, and the Lord shall descend,
A song in the night, oh my soul!

Glimpses & Reflections

1. What are the fears that have kept you from God's presence?

2. What are your hopes as you begin the process of growing closer to God?

3. What is one outcome you would be most excited about experiencing from growing closer to God? What was going on in your life where you felt closest to God?

CONCLUSION

At the end of my life, I don't want to look around and see people continuing to struggle in the valley and fail to find the next mountaintop because I didn't share the love and hope God has showered over me. It is my prayer that God brings my testimony to every heart who has been searching to rise from their pain. When our pain leads us to find God and ask Him the hard questions, the pain can be celebrated.

As we lay aside our hopelessness, anger, fear or feelings of "less than" and replace them with God's words, we will find He has been waiting there to heal us the whole time. We trade our sorrows for joy and desperation for hope. This is why we can boast in our weakness and be thankful for every trial. May each challenging climb teach us to live "greater than" we ever imagined.

In His service,

Janet

"Lord, I call out to you with all my heart. Answer me, and I will obey your orders. I call out to you. Save me, and I will keep your covenant laws. I get up before the sun rises. I cry out for help. I've put my hope in your word. My eyes stay open all night long. I spend my time thinking about your promises. Listen to me, because you love me. Lord, keep me alive as you have promised. Those who think up evil plans are near. They have wandered far away from your law. But Lord, you are near. All your commands are true. Long ago I learned from your covenant laws that you made them to last forever."
Psalm 119:145-153 NIRV

Glimpses & Reflections

1. As you conclude this study, what is your number one intention or strategy to help you rise during a challenge?

2. How have you experienced God at work in your life as you've gone through this book?

3. How can you begin to share these experiences with others?

ABOUT THE AUTHOR

Photo by Michelle Bourgeois

Janet Hines was raised on a farm near Indiana, Pennsylvania. As the oldest of five, she learned every aspect of hard work and farm life. Her roots grew deep into God's creation and the beauty of it which led to a passion for photography.

Through the combination of her photography, travel experiences and writing, she brings together pieces of life in ways that connect with the hurting people who need to know they are not alone. She writes about each of life's seasons, prayerfully bringing every reader to a closer relationship with God. Her heart's desire is to build a community of hope through sharing Christ all of her days.

In 2002, Janet co-founded Mi Esperanza, a ministry in Honduras focused on women's education. The program provides women with tangible, income-producing skills making them employable and capable of beginning their own business. You can find more information about this work at www.thewomenofmyhope.org.

Janet is on a journey of restoration, learning to be grateful for brokenness. She recognizes and celebrates that being shattered can sometimes be the perfect catalyst for driving us safely into the arms of Jesus.

JanetHines.com

CONNECT WITH JANET

Facebook: @JANETREEGER
Instagram: @jlikestogo

Email: janet@janethines.com

WORKS CITED

Holy Bible: New Living Translation. (2013) Carol Stream, IL: Tyndale House Publishers.

Lewis, C. S. The Collected Works of C.S. Lewis. New York: Inspirational Press, 1996.

New American Standard Bible: 1995 update. (1995). La Habra, CA: The Lockman Foundation.

New International Reader's Version. (1998). (1st ed). Zondervan.

Peterson, E. H. (2005). *The Message: the Bible in contemporary language.* Colorado Springs, CO: NavPress.

The Holy Bible: English Standard Version. (2016). Wheaton, IL: Crossway Bibles.

The Holy Bible: New International Version. (1984). Grand Rapids, MI: Zondervan.

Made in the USA
Monee, IL
26 December 2019